"*Winning with ADHD* is a powerful re   school, the home, and relationships. The playbook format is engaging, endearing, and so relatable. Grace's personal journey is an inspiration for teens everywhere."

—**Lara Honos-Webb, PhD**, author of *The ADHD Workbook for Teens*

"Grace Friedman and Sarah Cheyette have joined together to create the perfect playbook for attention deficit/hyperactivity disorder (ADHD). This book speaks directly to teens and young adults with ADHD from Grace's (a young adult with ADHD herself) perspective of knowing exactly what it's like to deal with and thrive with ADHD. Written in the style of a playbook for sports, it combines ADHD-specific 'plays' (which help readers break big tasks into smaller steps) with concepts to better understand ADHD and guidance on making wise choices that those without ADHD never have to make. It is full of straight talk from the authors and other teens about managing ADHD and winning and thriving personally, at home, in school, and with friends. Readers will immediately feel understood while being coached and encouraged to make changes that lead to creating the life they want."

—**Debra Burdick, LCSW**, author of *Mindfulness for Teens with ADHD* and *ADHD*

"*Winning with ADHD* is a truly extraordinary book for teens with ADHD. Written by a young woman with ADHD who has clearly walked the walk, every page is filled with warmth and wisdom. It covers all the important aspects for teens to know about ADHD—from understanding the diagnosis to self-care, medications, and specific strategies for conquering the challenges that arise at school, at home, and with friends. Practical advice is buoyed by real-life examples and heartfelt optimism. This book affirms, guides, and inspires; and most of all it gives hope to the many teens struggling with ADHD. *Winning with ADHD* is a grand slam!"

> —**Linda Pfiffner, PhD**, professor in residence and
> director of the hyperactivity attention and learning
> problems program in the department of psychiatry at
> the Weill Institute for Neurosciences at the University
> of California, San Francisco

"Wow, a book that is written for teens with ADHD, not about them or at them—in other words, a book that they will actually read. Most of. Okay, some of them. But still. And they will be so much better off for spending some time with this gem, since the better they understand themselves, ADHD and all, the more successful and happier they will be. (You will also be happier, but don't tell your teen that.)"

> —**Ari Tuckman, PsyD, MBA**, psychologist, author,
> public speaker, advocate, and ADHD expert

"This book for teens is refreshingly honest and practical. It provides kids with relatable situations and no-nonsense advice. I especially like the section on controlling the controllable things in life. When kids feel overwhelmed or frustrated, they will learn what they can focus on so that they can feel more in control and better able to manage their challenges."

—**Cindy Goldrich, EdM, ADHD-CCSP**, parent coach, teacher trainer, founder of PTS Coaching, and author of *8 Keys to Parenting Children with ADHD* and the video *Executive Function, ADHD, and Stress in the Classroom*

"The combination of an author who has ADHD plus a pediatric neurologist who specializes in it packs twice the effectiveness in one book. Friedman presents her own experiences to the reader, while Cheyette provides the research. The book is written in a format that is palatable to people who may have found other books on ADHD a challenge to read through."

—**Stephanie Sarkis, PhD**, author of *Natural Relief for Adult ADHD* and *10 Simple Solutions to Adult ADD*

"*Winning with ADHD* speaks directly to teens with positive, practical help for key challenges—from study habits to managing depression. It's a winner!"

—**Katherine Ellison**, Pulitzer Prize-winning journalist and author of *Buzz*

"In *Winning with ADHD*, Grace Friedman and Sarah Cheyette show adolescents how to take ownership of their ADHD, their brains, and their behavior with positivity and encouragement. Full of compassion, clarity, and kindness, the authors normalize living with ADHD and help teens acknowledge their challenges while showing them how to accomplish goals and succeed in life. Friedman's refreshing honesty about her own experience, and Cheyette's professional insight and clinical examples ground the book's information and useful suggestions in real-life examples of change and success. *Winning with ADHD* is a must-read for teens, their families, and professionals!"

> —**Sharon Saline**, licensed clinical psychologist with more than twenty-five years' experience empowering children and teens with ADHD and executive function challenges, and author of *What Your ADHD Child Wishes You Knew*

"So many wonderful strategies in *Winning with ADHD*! A great guide for any student looking for practical, implementable tips. The combination of Sarah's expert advice and Grace's real-life strategies make this book a terrific resource."

> —**Ana Homayoun**, author of *That Crumpled Paper Was Due Last Week*

winning
with **adhd**

a playbook for **teens** &
young adults with
attention deficit/
hyperactivity disorder

GRACE FRIEDMAN
SARAH CHEYETTE, MD

Instant Help Books
An Imprint of New Harbinger Publications, Inc.

Publisher's Note

This publication is designed to provide accurate and authoritative information in regard to the subject matter covered. It is sold with the understanding that the publisher is not engaged in rendering psychological, financial, legal, or other professional services. If expert assistance or counseling is needed, the services of a competent professional should be sought.

Distributed in Canada by Raincoast Books

Copyright © 2019 by Grace Friedman and Sarah Cheyette
Instant Help Books
An imprint of New Harbinger Publications, Inc.
5674 Shattuck Avenue
Oakland, CA 94609
www.newharbinger.com

Cover design by Amy Shoup

Acquired by Jess O'Brien

Edited by Kristi Hein

Library of Congress Cataloging-in-Publication Data on file

21   20   19

10   9   8   7   6   5   4   3   2   1   First Printing

Contents

Foreword

Everyone has opinions about ADHD these days. Most scientists and evidence-based clinicians rightfully believe that it's a biologically based condition affecting an individual's focus, attention, and self-regulation—and that engagement in treatment and self-management can help the individual thrive. But others believe that it's a hoax—the product of unresponsive classrooms, a society hell-bent on achievement at all costs (and at ever earlier ages), or a clamoring for performance-enhancing medications. Or that it's solely a U.S. condition, unknown in the rest of the world. Still others contend that ADHD is nothing other than a series of hidden strengths, meaning that it shouldn't be considered a "disorder" at all. A subgroup promotes a range of unsubstantiated remedies—homeopathy, herbs, extreme diets, supplements, and the like—that they claim can free people from ADHD, dismissing evidence-based medication and psychosocial interventions.

Countless articles and books have been written on the entire topic. Voluminous websites and social media posts espouse multiple, conflicting perspectives, yielding a torrent of information and, too often, misinformation. Little wonder that things get polarized rather than synthesized.

But in the midst of such contention, imagine an energetic, optimistic, yet realistic young woman with a history of ADHD, who tells fundamental truths about her life and the condition with which she copes, while offering some of the most sound and authentic tips and coaching points one could imagine. That's what Grace Friedman has done in *Winning with ADHD,* with able mentoring provided by Sarah Cheyette.

To call this work refreshing is an understatement, though it is indeed a welcome break from many of the "one size fits all" self-help workbooks found in bookstores and libraries, and online. Even more, the book is practical, candid, wise (it's hard to believe that Grace is only recently a college graduate), authoritative without being preachy, appropriately humorous when needed, and— over and above all these attributes—deep. After an authentic, colloquial, and humanizing introduction to herself and her long-standing issues with ADHD, Grace addresses the crucial issue of accepting the diagnosis before diving into self-care and self-management, home-related issues, school problems and coping strategies, peer struggles, and treatment-related facts and strategies, particularly surrounding ADHD medications. The prose is engaging, and the strategies are rooted in understandable steps. I can say that I have never witnessed a more *relatable* book on the topic than *Winning with ADHD.*

Among the many wonderful features of this work, one of the most telling is that Grace is fully cognizant of the difficulties in core life domains incurred by ADHD. At the same time, she is completely convinced that many of the attributes exhibited by those with the condition can be advantageous, so long as major coping strategies are engaged. In other words, the book is a major step forward in integrating the "unrelenting disorder" versus "hidden strength" dichotomy that so often prevents needed synthesis and perspective.

I first met Grace a number of years ago when she and her father attended a talk I gave in Northern California on myths and realities linked to ADHD. Following my presentation, she eagerly spoke with me about her dream of providing crucial resources for teens with ADHD, everywhere. The blend of enthusiasm and dedication I saw in her eyes was remarkable. Indeed, it still is.

All too rare, in my experience, are books that come from the heart, blending core experiences with evidence-based practices as they speak directly to teens and young adults with conditions like ADHD. I believe that the candor and authenticity permeating these pages will play a major (if not directly intended) role in destigmatizing the entire condition. Shame and self-blame are instantly removed from the equation in the honest, basic, and deeply human language each chapter comprises. I believe that no one can emerge from reading this book without understanding the essential humanity of everyone dealing with ADHD.

Winning with ADHD is a needed, life-enhancing, eminently readable and relatable work. Its common sense nature belies its depth and humanity. I'm honored to introduce readers to this exceptional book.

—Stephen P. Hinshaw, PhD

Professor of Psychology, University of California, Berkeley

Author, *Another Kind of Madness: A Journey through Stigma and Hope of Mental Illness*

introduction

OMG, I Have ADHD?

We know exactly how you feel.

Did someone buy you this book to read? Maybe your parents? School counselor? Therapist? You probably find reading a whole book pretty challenging sometimes. So why should you read this one?

Let us answer that with a little story:

This girl is walking down the street when she falls into a hole. The walls are so steep she can't get out.

A doctor passes by, and the girl shouts up, "Hey, Doc. Can you help me out?" The doctor writes a prescription for some ADHD medication, throws it down to her, and moves on.

Then a judge comes along, and the girl shouts up, "Judge, I'm down in this hole! Can you help me out?" The judge writes out an order for some accommodations at her school, throws it down into the hole, and moves on.

Then her friend walks by. "Hey, Grace, it's me! Can you help me out?"

I jump down into the hole.

Our girl says, "Grace...are you stupid? Now we're both down here."

I say, "Yeah, but I've been down here before, and I know the way out."

How did you feel when you first learned you had ADHD? Did your doctor teach you how to manage it?

For teens and young adults with ADHD, so many things that others consider easy we find challenging, frustrating, and at times overwhelming. There are prescriptions to help us focus. There are laws to provide us with accommodations. Unfortunately, the many professionals in our lives—doctors, therapists, teachers, coaches, and even clergy—often don't teach us how to get out of this hole.

Want to get out? We will jump down in there with you and show you how.

This is what you need to know first:

- *You can* be hugely successful—and *win* in life—with your ADHD. In fact, tapping into "your ADHD"—rather than denying it—is key.

- Winning with ADHD requires *you* to accept it, own it, manage it, and learn to adapt.

- Winning with ADHD requires practice—just like becoming a great musician, athlete, mathematician, astronaut...OK, you get the point. Practice, practice, practice. This books gives you the "plays" to practice to become a *winner.*

Let's get introduced. We are Grace and Dr. Sarah.

I am Grace, and I have ADHD. As we write this book, I am just twenty-one. I have a severe case of ADHD. I am both very inattentive and very hyperactive. I learned about my ADHD when I was just twelve and felt like I was wearing a very heavy backpack full of rocks. I hated these rocks, and I wanted to get rid of them, but I couldn't find anyone who could explain to me, in a language I could understand, what I needed to do to lighten my heavy load. That was really frustrating.

As a result, I became passionate about wanting to help others with ADHD. So when I was just fifteen, I published my first book, *Embracing Your ADHD*, to help teens with ADHD just like you understand the three key points just listed. Since then, I coach kids with ADHD, work with therapists and doctors who treat ADHD, speak to parents of kids with ADHD, write about ADHD, and—having learned to manage my ADHD—I just graduated college, on a scholarship and with honors.

Dr. Sarah is a pediatric neurologist and an expert in working with kids with ADHD. Dr. Sarah has treated thousands of kids like me and has helped their families understand those three crucial points. She knows how the minds and bodies of ADHD teens work. She also writes about ADHD in her other book, *ADHD and the Focused Mind*, with the goal of helping young people with ADHD learn to become independent, strong, and successful.

We, Grace and Dr. Sarah, decided to team up on this book with one goal in mind: teaching you how to win with ADHD. Just like learning how to play a new sport or musical instrument, learning how to win with ADHD requires a lot of practice. It requires taking instruction, learning new ideas, hard work, patience, and perseverance.

It's easier to learn a new sport when you are on a team. It's easier to learn a new instrument when you are in a band or an orchestra. It's easier when you know you are part of a group, all learning and trying hard to get better together. Being a part of a group makes learning how to win with ADHD easier too. You are not alone: you are part of a group, a team.

Most teams have a name, so we are going to call you ADDYTeens. When you read *ADDYTeens* in this book, we are talking to the whole team of young people with ADHD—millions of us, all around the world—and you are part of that team.

You Are Not Alone—We Are All ADDYTeens!

I felt that the worst part of having ADHD was feeling alone, isolated, and different from my friends. It took a while, but I realized that there are millions of kids—just like you, just like me—who have ADHD. Most everyone hides it. Most everyone is ashamed to talk about it. I learned that many of my friends have ADHD, some of my teachers have ADHD, and ADHD runs in my family.

So why be ashamed? Why hide your ADHD? When I started working as an advocate for young people with ADHD, I wanted to break the stigma of ADHD so many seem to have. I wanted to spark a conversation and create a community, and to focus everyone's attention on what young people with ADHD really need to learn to manage their ADHD, embrace it, thrive with it, and, yes, *win* with ADHD.

After realizing that I was not alone with my diagnosis, I created the moniker "ADDYTeen" to represent every kid who has ADHD and establish an inclusive ADHD community. Adults label us, and adults speak about us, so I felt it was time we took control of this conversation.

I set up my website, www.addyteen.com, to create a sense of place where ADDYTeens can share their experiences.

What does it mean to have ADHD? What does it take to thrive with ADHD? What does it take to explain what ADHD is like to those who don't know? What do you need to know about ADHD to make the changes in your life that will ultimately help you get to your chosen destination?

Join the conversation! This book will help you answer all these questions and take control over your life with ADHD. It's your life, even if you are just twelve or thirteen. It's time to take control and make things happen!

Winning with ADHD

Let's be honest: having ADHD can be a drag. Literally. Having ADHD is, again, like having to carry a backpack full of heavy rocks wherever you go, when most of your friends and family do not. Bummer, right?

Yes—and no.

Three things about ADHD are true, and the sooner you accept them, the more likely it is you will be able to learn how to win in life on your terms.

- ADHD is a real thing. It's a medical condition. It is how you were born. You did not choose to have it, you did not do anything wrong, and it will not go away if you ignore it. In fact, it never goes away. Yup, real talk. However, learning to manage ADHD can make you very strong, creative, competitive, and accomplished. Think about it. Who is stronger: those who have learned how to thrive carrying a heavy backpack filled with rocks, or those who have never had to carry one?

- You are not alone. There are millions of young people who have ADHD. It's nothing to be ashamed of. You are not stupid, you are not weak, you do not have a defect. But it is a challenge, no doubt. Life is unfair; having ADHD is unfair. Get comfortable with this idea.

- Having ADHD just means you think differently, you process information differently, and you do things differently. This means you will learn differently and succeed using different techniques from those without ADHD. That's right; you will need to manage your ADHD, or it will manage you.

Now do yourself a favor, and read those three points again. This is what our book is about. Winning with ADHD means:

- You need to accept who you are.

- You need to recognize that you're not alone.

- You need to learn how to adapt when necessary in order to thrive.

What Does Winning Mean to You?

When you are a little kid, your parents have to tell you what to do. You don't know; you're just a little kid. By the time you're an adult and in college, you should be responsible for getting things done. You shouldn't need parents to tell you what to do.

Now, in your teenage years, you are in between—you are not a little kid, and you are not an adult. You are on a journey to becoming independent, responsible, and capable. This is a great time to sort out what you do and do not want for yourself. Here are some things to think about:

- What do you value?

- What are your strengths?

- What parts of your life need to be better developed?

- Which of those might you need a little help developing?

Sometimes people (parents, coaches) have ideas about what you should be doing. You may or may not buy into those ideas. However, you may want to consider them. They may be good ideas. Everyone benefits from coaching and help at times, and it can be good for you to have someone outside yourself looking at what you are doing and trying to help you set goals.

Here is what you need to know:

- Can you look yourself in the mirror—look right into your own eyes—and believe in what you are doing?

- Do you know what winning means to *you*?

These are your choices. You need to start making these decisions and, as you do, learn how to work past the challenges your ADHD presents. It's not anyone else's choice. Maybe your parents want you to get all A's, but you are happy enough with a few B's sprinkled in so you can do your football practice five days a week. Maybe your coach wants you to be the best basketball player you could be, but there are too many practices, and they interfere with that tutoring job you love. You need to define what *you* want, and go for it. Keep in mind, there will be bumps along the way. Buckle up.

Let's Hear from ADDYTeens

Samira, seventeen, always thought she was going to be a scientist, in part because both her parents were scientists, and it was always assumed that Samira would follow in their footsteps. Every year in high school she really tried to devote herself to science, taking honors classes in biology and studying hard for the SAT subject tests. However, in her senior year she loved her journalism elective, and she decided: *This is it. This is what I want to do.* It was really hard to break the news to her parents, and she had to really scramble to write the articles, as she tended to procrastinate until the deadline, but she was much happier writing than doing lab work.

Let's Hear from You!

What are your goals? Your aspirations?

What are the steps to get there?

What are you willing to do to reach your dreams?

What will you have to do differently from what you are doing now?

Did you know that other young people with ADHD learn to do well in school, at sports, at work—and even write books?

Many famous and well-known individuals have "won" with ADHD, including Justin Timberlake, Richard Branson, and Michael Phelps. They've all succeeded phenomenally.

Concepts, Coaching, and Choices

As you read this book, you'll learn how to win with "Your ADHD"—to take control in your life, achieve your aspirations, and pursue your dreams with confidence, competitiveness, and capability. We have organized this book into three sections:

- Concepts
- Coaching
- Choices

You can't manage something you don't understand—and with our *concepts*, we help you understand how the minds and bodies of ADDYTeens work.

Our *coaching* helps you break down big tasks into smaller steps so you can deal with all the life challenges (challenges that are a little bit more difficult with ADHD). Just as you learn how to practice soccer drills, dance routines, or moves in martial arts, our step-by-step *Plays* teach you how to tackle ADHD-related challenges in a way that becomes fluid and natural.

With *choices*, we break down and simplify the decisions ADDYTeens have to make in middle school, high school, and eventually college. ADDYTeens must make many choices that kids without ADHD never have to make. We ADDYTeens need to advocate for ourselves, get resources we need to succeed, and make sure we stay on the right track to accomplish our goals and dreams. There are many choices, and you have to make these for yourself.

Concepts, coaching, and choices, all together, help frame what it's like to live with ADHD, the adjustments and growth required to thrive with ADHD, and the steps we need to take to embrace and win with our ADHD.

Think About It   Any challenge in life requires you to try hard, even if you don't think you'll perform well at first.

Learning and Using the Plays

This book is about change—making changes in your life to help you work past your challenges, exploit your strengths, and accomplish your goals. You need coaching for this, just like you need coaches in soccer or basketball, music teachers, and dance instructors, and you need to learn and practice to become skilled and accomplished.

Our Plays are step-by-step instructions to learn skills that relate to your ADHD. There are two types: Foundational Plays and Set Plays.

Foundational Plays teach you a basic skill that you can use in many situations. Every ADDYTeen needs to learn these—no exceptions. Some examples are managing your time, speaking up for yourself, and managing your emotions. Think about soccer: before "newbie" players can compete in a game, they must first learn the basic skills of dribbling and kicking the ball with the left and right foot and how to throw the ball in.

Set Plays apply to specific situations that ADDYTeens frequently face, in which they draw on the basic Foundation Plays they have learned. For example, preparing for a test requires managing your time; working out issues at home requires speaking up for yourself.

Just like in soccer, a Set Play relates to a situation that you can anticipate will happen and need to prepare for in advance, practicing it over and over so when you are in that situation—such as a penalty or corner kick—you are prepared to do your very best.

Think About It Here is the real question: What do you want out of your life?

Yes, ADHD is challenging to manage. And yes, ADHD is frustrating to deal with. OK, ADHD is a pain in the butt—yup, we said it.

> But, no, ADHD is not debilitating. ADHD will not prevent you from accomplishing your goals, doing great things, and succeeding in life.
>
> Only you can do that. So...don't do that!
>
> Focus on winning. You can, and you should.

Suit Up

My dad always told me, "You can't win if you don't suit up." And you know what? He is totally right. To win in life, and to manage your ADHD to the best of your ability, you need to adapt to your ADHD, not the other way around. You need to be active in the game, too. Not just suited up to play; you need to be involved and invested in whatever you are doing. This includes managing your ADHD.

For me, ADHD seemed like a big scary monster that I didn't know how to live with. So how could I learn to manage it? I really wanted to win, so I decided I had to suit up and get to work managing my ADHD, practicing, learning, and working hard at it.

Same for you: to win, you must suit up, then start practicing. Easy to say, but hard for many ADDYTeens. But we are here to help you get out of the hole.

This book is your starting place!

My starting place was a point when I was sick and tired of spending three hours on homework that took my friends only thirty minutes to complete. *Listen, take notes, look at the board, remember the lecture, apply the lecture to my homework.* It was just too much! I didn't remember the class material I learned in school, and I was always frustrated and angry and didn't know how to voice my thoughts and feelings. Even when I found myself stuck, I didn't know how to ask for help. I felt ashamed. I didn't want to speak up in class asking what I feared were stupid questions. I was afraid of becoming an outcast.

I knew I had to make a change—but where would I start? With the basics!

We've talked about the need to learn the basics in soccer, basketball, or any other sport. Before you can be a champion, you need to start with basic skills like dribbling the ball, shooting, passing, and defending. You also have to work on basic conditioning so you have the stamina to play through a full game. You don't have to be the best at these skills—just as in sports, there will always be someone better (or worse) than you are. But you can always achieve your personal best.

Control the Controllables

When you face a challenging situation—for example, preparing for a big test, taking the SAT, getting ready to perform in theater, or performing in a music recital—many things are happening all at once. To be successful, you first have to learn how to face and tackle challenges. Everyone does. For ADDYTeens like us, facing challenges requires extra work. Life with ADHD takes extra work. Is this fair? Heck no.

Think About It   Have you ever felt stuck, defeated, or frustrated? Are there situations that are challenging for you? What are they?

So, managing your ADHD using our Plays is not about your flaws; it's about practicing how to do your best work based on your capabilities. In fact, right now, stop thinking about your ADHD as a flaw. Instead, recognize that ADHD is just the way you think. You can learn to improve how you think and do things, just as you can improve how you throw a football or shoot a basket. It just takes time. It also takes control.

How do you get started? Here is how I got started. I learned to control the controllables. Perhaps you are wondering *Uhhh... What is a* controllable?

In essence, a controllable is any aspect of life that you have some power to control. First, get clear on what is *not* a controllable. What can't you control? We cannot control every detail, event, or action in our lives. We don't control what others do, we don't control traffic or the weather; we can only control our attitude and our actions.

That bears repeating. *You can only control your attitude and actions.* Ta-da!

I learned this important lesson—*control the controllables*—at a soccer training camp at UC Berkeley. I trained with college and professional players as a goalkeeper. The goalkeeper is responsible for trying to block every single shot from entering the goal. Let one in and the game is changed. The goalkeeper is the last person to stop an attack, to prevent the other team from scoring.

Not an easy position. Being a striker or a midfielder requires more running, but it's way less pressure. When a striker or midfielder does not block or make their shot, the game is not changed. The score remains the same.

Here is what I needed to know: a goalkeeper will face fifteen to thirty shots on goal per game, and some of these will get by. I had to learn to accept that there were shots I could not block. Goals would be scored, no matter what I did. I couldn't control what others did, or the condition of the field, or the weather, or the wind. I could only control the controllables.

Remember: even when the goalie is scored on, the game plays on. The goalkeeper can't lose focus; the goalkeeper can't just quit; the game is still on. As goalkeeper, I had to control what I *could*— my attitude and my actions. This lesson led directly to the process I invented for myself to learn to manage my ADHD. I knew I could not work perfectly all the time; I would make some mistakes. Sometimes I did better; other times I did worse.

What does this mean for you? Focus only on what you can control.

- Your attitude—will you be positive or negative?

- Your actions—will you be productive or ineffectual?

- Your time—will you use it wisely or waste it?

- Your emotions—will you manage them or let them manage you?

Anything other than that is out of your reach. Let it go.

Many people with ADHD become anxious because they are trying to control too much.

Step by step, you control what you can, when you can, to the best of your abilities. Slowing things down, thinking about the next step, and controlling what comes to you is called *process*. The Plays in this book are processes. Learn them! Practice them! Repeat them until they become natural. Like riding a bike. Like shooting a basket. Like dribbling a soccer ball. Like playing catch.

Like feeling like a winner.

As you read, you can take action to manage your ADHD. The first step is *you* deciding to do something. Deciding is the first step. Taking action means you stop worrying and start doing! It's easier to take action if you have specific steps to follow. We are here to help. When you see Take Action boxes, it's time to get busy!

Take Action

1. Write down what *you* want from reading this book. How do you envision yourself winning?

2. If it sounds scary or unreachable, make a set of smaller goals.

3. Post what you wrote in a prominent place where you will see it. It will help keep you on track!

chapter 1

You and Your ADHD

OK. You have just heard that you have ADHD. Hearing that diagnosis can create different emotions. However you feel is OK.

Think About It   How did you feel after receiving your ADHD diagnosis?

Some ADDYTeens feel powerless and hopeless, as if they will never be able to succeed. Others respond with relief, learning that there is a real issue they face and they are not just "lazy." Some keep their ADHD diagnosis a secret. Others can't wait to finally tell their family, friends, and teachers about their ADHD in hopes of feeling validated.

Were you disappointed? Relieved? Something else?

Whatever you felt, one thing is certain—the better you understand your ADHD, the better you can manage it. So let's start with terminology. Many are confused by the difference between ADD and ADHD. Some think ADD means "I'm not hyper," and that ADHD means "I am hyper." Actually, there is no longer an official ADD diagnosis. It's *all* called ADHD.

- Calm but inattentive people are diagnosed "ADHD—predominantly inattentive."

- Physically hyperactive people are diagnosed "ADHD—predominantly hyperactive."

- Those who—like me!—have features of both groups are diagnosed "ADHD—combined."

Here is a better question: what does it mean to think in an ADHD way? Well, to understand that, you first must understand what it means to think in a focused way.

- When you think in a focused way, your brain sees one thing as more important than others.

- When you think in an ADHD way—in an unfocused way—there is not just one thought in your head that stands out. Your brain "sees" a lot of different thoughts at once. So your brain skips from one thing to the other.

Thinking in an ADHD way can actually be helpful! Thinking about multiple ideas at once can help you connect your thoughts together and see the bigger picture. But not all the time.

With ADHD, focus is less automatic than it should be. ADHD doesn't mean you can't focus, but you have difficulty with automatically focusing. ADHD makes it harder to stick with and complete a task—like your homework, or cleaning your room, or finishing a project. Your brain jumps from one task to the other, sometimes jumping back, sometimes losing track of what you were doing.

For example, now that you are focusing on reading this book, your brain should be thinking about just the words on this page. Your brain should see the words on this page as more important than all the other things your brain could be paying attention to—the pictures on your walls, what your friend said to you yesterday, or your phone.

If you are thinking in an unfocused or ADHD way, your brain may start with the words on this page, but then you might also start thinking about other things. You might notice that a picture on the wall isn't quite straight, and then get up to straighten it, and while you are up you notice that you left something on your bookshelf that you wanted to give to your friend. Then you might remember *another* friend you wanted to talk with, and you go over and call her.

Yep, your brain started with the words on the page, but instead of that remaining more important than other thoughts or items around you, you got distracted and stopped reading.

Now you know why it takes you so long to do your homework!

ADDYTeens describe this feeling in different ways: "It's like my brain is playing six radios at once," or "My brain never stops." ADHD brains are frequently looking for something new—some new stimulus—hopping from one thing to the other. So ADDYTeens often complain they are easily bored if there is not enough stimulus around. On the other hand, sometimes it might feel like you are thinking about nothing; the task you are supposed to be doing flies out of your brain and is replaced by—well, not much.

Think About It Despite what you may have heard, people cannot actually multitask (pay attention to and do more than one thing at a time). So you can't actually do homework while watching TV. It might *feel* like you can do two things at once, but actually you are shifting from one to the other, often so fast you don't even realize what you are doing. Your brain may start with homework, then go to TV, then back to homework, then back to TV, and so on. The problem is, when you shift focus back and forth like this, you make more mistakes. Your brain is constantly refocusing and asking, *Where was I? What was I doing?*

Hello! It takes longer to do two tasks "at once" than it does to do one, finish, then do the other. And it is more stressful. So put your phone down and read this book. *Just kidding!* But no, really.

What Does Having ADHD Mean for You?

Dr. Sarah diagnoses young people (and, yes, adults too!) who may have ADHD by using a handbook that describes the symptoms of various mental health conditions. It's called the *Diagnostic and Statistical Manual of Mental Disorders,* or *DSM-V* (V meaning it's the fifth edition). If you meet the criteria, then you qualify for an ADHD diagnosis. There are two categories of criteria: *inattention* and *hyperactivity.*

Inattention: People with ADHD show a persistent pattern of inattention that interferes with functioning or development. The *DSM-V* lists these:

- Often fails to give close attention to details or makes careless mistakes in schoolwork, at work, or with other activities.

- Often has trouble holding attention on tasks or play activities.

- Often does not seem to listen when spoken to directly.

- Often does not follow through on instructions and fails to finish schoolwork, chores, or duties in the workplace (for example, loses focus, sidetracked).

- Often has trouble organizing tasks and activities.

- Often avoids, dislikes, or is reluctant to do tasks that require mental effort over a long period of time (such as school work or homework).

- Often loses things necessary for tasks and activities (such as school materials, pencils, books, tools, wallets, keys, paperwork, eyeglasses, mobile phones).

- Is often easily distracted.

- Is often forgetful in daily activities.

You don't have to meet all of these criteria. If you are under seventeen, you have to meet six to have a diagnosis of ADHD, inattentive. If you are seventeen and over, meeting five is enough.

Note, the word "often" in the criteria is key; if it wasn't there, just about everyone would be diagnosed!

How many of the inattention criteria ring true for you? Most of them? Or only a few of them? If the latter, maybe your ADHD is predominantly hyperactive. Let's look at those criteria.

Hyperactivity and Impulsivity: People with ADHD show patterns of hyperactivity-impulsivity that interfere with functioning or development. The *DSM-V* lists these:

- Often fidgets with or taps hands or feet, or squirms in seat.

- Often leaves seat in situations when remaining seated is expected.

- Often runs about or climbs in situations where it is not appropriate (adolescents or adults may be limited to feeling restless).

- Often unable to play or take part in leisure activities quietly.

- Is often "on the go," acting as if "driven by a motor."

- Often talks excessively.

- Often blurts out an answer before a question has been completed.

- Often has trouble waiting his/her turn.

- Often interrupts or intrudes on others (for example, butts into conversations or games).

Being hyperactive means feeling compelled to be extremely active—you find it really hard to stay seated, or you *feel* you have to move a lot. Remember, being fidgety is not enough to qualify you as hyperactive. Again, to meet the diagnostic criteria, you need six of these if you are under seventeen, and five if you are seventeen and older, and "often" is also key here.

"Combined type ADHD" means that you meet criteria for both categories.

Here are some important details. You can't have ADHD for just a few months, or for just one subject. To be diagnosed, ADHD symptoms must be present for over six months, and they have to be significant; for example, you don't just forget a few things now and then—you forget things a *lot*. Your ADHD symptoms also must be present in different settings. You can't just have them in biology class; they must be present both at home and at school.

Bottom line: everybody thinks in a focused way sometimes, and everybody thinks in an ADHD way sometimes. But if you think in an ADHD way most of the time, enough so that it affects how you perform both in school and at home, you get diagnosed with ADHD.

Dr. Sarah notes that although these criteria may sound pretty bad, ADHD has good aspects too. For example, ADDYTeens can be super creative, super fun, super energetic in a good way, and super bright.

ADHD Is Just Part of Your Biology

Researchers know something about the biology of ADHD—but not that much. We know that ADHD tends to run in families, so it's somewhat "genetic." That means your grandparents, parents, siblings, uncles, aunts, and cousins may also have ADHD—even if they do not know it or have a diagnosis. Our genes are tiny, incredibly important building blocks of our body that are transferred from parents to their children and determine some characteristics of the child. When you inherit a characteristic from your parents—for example, your eye, hair, and skin color—it's called "genetic." Some medical conditions—including ADHD—are also genetic.

When I was diagnosed with ADHD, I learned soon after that my dad also has ADHD. I say "has," not "had," because his ADHD has not gone away; he just learned how to manage it and use his strengths to his advantage. Hearing about his personal experiences with ADHD as a young boy and how his ADHD changed as an adult was inspiring. Learning about my dad's ADHD helped me accept and move forward with my diagnosis. It also taught me that my ADHD does not have to hold me back; over time I could learn to manage it.

ADHD Is Not an Illness

Not every medical condition is an illness. People who need glasses have a medical condition, but they are not ill. Heads up, ADDYTeens! Having ADHD does not mean you are ill, or sick, or broken. It's wrong to think of ADHD as an illness. Even though medication can be involved, you are not mentally ill. Medication for ADHD is kind of like glasses or contact lenses—it doesn't heal or cure a disorder, but it can help you function better. Glasses help your eyes focus, and you can choose to wear them or not.

Glasses don't make you smart, and nearsightedness or farsightedness does not make you dumb either.

Do you think your friends who wear glasses are ill, or sick, or broken? No way.

Medical terms like *disorder* or *disease* or *syndrome* are used for serious medical conditions like diabetes, cancer, and sickle-cell anemia. ADHD is sometimes called a disorder or a syndrome, depending on individual differences in biology. Unfortunately, diagnostic labels can have an impact on how individuals view themselves and how others view the individual. Just think of ADHD as a medical condition, which, like impaired eyesight, may require changing how you do things.

Think About It   Words like *disease* and *disorder* sound really bad. How does it make you feel to be told you have a disorder? Do you feel ashamed? What if you thought of your diagnosis not as a disorder, but as simply a part of the way you think?

If you're anything like me, sometimes you think in a focused way, and sometimes you think in an ADHD way. Just as with other personality traits, such as optimism or a silly personality, no one thinks in an ADHD way all the time. Sometimes the ADHD part of your thinking is prominent, and at times that may be OK—even great! The trick—and one of the main goals of this book—is to explain and teach ADDY Teens like us when we should let our energetic and creative sides out and when we need to focus our energy in a productive way.

> ADHD is always a part of how we think and behave. This book will help you practice and determine the best way to act in a given situation.

Medical terminology used for ADHD can sometimes make us feel somehow broken. Dr. Sarah and I believe it doesn't really matter what you call it; it's how you think about it that matters. There are some good things about ADHD, and there are some difficult things about ADHD. Don't overthink it.

ADHD versus Asthma: Similarities and Differences

For years, I played on a traveling academy soccer team that was extremely demanding both physically and mentally. For practice and games, each team member had to be prepared in order for the team to have the best shot at winning.

Several of the players had asthma. Asthma is a medical condition that makes it hard to breath sometimes. Before each practice and game, they had to use their inhaler to ensure they could breathe well for hours while running.

I played goalkeeper, so I was the last line of defense. I definitely needed to be focused at all times. I was the only team member with ADHD. I had to remember to take my ADHD medication before heading onto the field to ensure that I would be as attentive as possible.

The girls with asthma and I both had to take extra steps to be physically and mentally able to perform at our best. However, sometimes my coaches questioned my use of ADHD medication before the games. The coaches told me, "Just try harder—just concentrate!" They never told the asthmatic girls, "Just try harder—just breathe right!" Asthma medication and ADHD medication are no different, if you think about it: both are used to help someone function better. So why would the people who need to use them be treated differently?

Think About It Think of a time when you've had a really bad case of the flu. You feel awful, flat on your back in bed with a fever and aches, a stuffed head, maybe a hacking cough. Family and friends come to help you, offering you soup and get-well wishes: "Feel better soon!" But imagine if they treated a flu like they often treat ADHD. Imagine your family and friends saying, "Why don't you just try harder not to have the flu? Maybe if you just change your attitude a bit, then you won't have the flu!" What the heck? Why would anyone think that a condition like ADHD is any less real or challenging than having any other condition? Maybe it's because we really can't see what is going on in our brain. At least with the flu, although the virus is invisible, the yucky cough, sneezing, and fever are all obvious to everyone.

ADDYTeens often face discussions about whether they have something "real" or not. Many people without ADHD have no problem with sitting still or focusing when they choose to, so it's hard for them to understand why for some it is not a simple matter of choosing.

With asthma, you don't have to take lung function tests in front of all your friends. With ADHD, you are "graded" every day in front of your peers, parents, and teachers. When you don't bring what you need to soccer practice, everyone notices. When you don't make eye contact with people who are talking to you because your mind is elsewhere, everyone notices—they get offended.

It's rare for anyone to get frustrated if someone with asthma forgets to use their inhaler.

Historically, because the brain has been so mysterious, issues that affect it have been harder to quantify as truly biological. We know a lot more about how other organs function than how the brain works. In general, any behavior that involves a connection with your brain is not well understood, so people often assume you can control everything your brain does. With a fever, you can measure it. With a broken bone, you can x-ray it. With anemia, you can do a blood test. With ADHD—well, at this point, we can't see it in the brain at all.

When the soccer game is over, no one cares who used their inhaler and who used their ADHD medication. All the team cares about is who suited up and who performed well in the game. Your ADHD medication is like soccer cleats: it gives you the traction you need to play well. It is *not* like performance-enhancing steroids, drugs designed to give you an edge over others. Your medication just brings you up to your own "normal" level. It helps you play to win.

The Nature of the Race: Problems versus Challenges

Have you ever seen a track race? Remember the analogy in the introduction about ADHD being like wearing a backpack full of rocks? Suppose one of the runners had the backpack full of rocks—would you expect them to finish first? Not likely. Now answer this: was she a loser, given that she had to run the race with all that extra weight? Nope. Absolutely not.

If you regularly run races with a heavy backpack, you'll get stronger and stronger. There are definitely some disadvantages to being the runner with the heavy backpack, but weakness is not one of them. After all those super-conditioning races, you will be stronger in ways that will be truly valuable in your life.

Who crosses the finish line first does not reflect who worked the hardest to complete the race, or who is the strongest runner. Think of this in the context of school. Does the person with the best grades always become the most successful adult? As you'll find out after you attend a few high school reunions: heck no! What matters are the skills and strategies you create over the years and later in life. These strategies will help you run your race with more ease and enthusiasm.

Some people describe their ADHD as a problem. Problems can be really hard or impossible to fix—like being blind or paralyzed. Challenges are different; they take work to sort out, but they can be fixed. It is best to think of ADHD as a challenge that you can meet and manage, rather than a problem that you can't really fix. Do you think the runner with the heavy backpack has a problem—or a challenge? How does that make you feel about your ADHD?

Winning sometimes means trying and failing over and over, but never giving up. Life is complicated. You are never going to be the best at everything. That doesn't mean you stop trying to become better. Remember: you can't run your race if you don't suit up and start. Challenges need to be faced. ADHD is not a problem; it's a challenge.

Let's Hear from ADDYTeens

Jason, seventeen, never did get the hang of taking tests in high school. He tended to make a lot of errors on multiple-choice tests. However, he developed great ways to study so that he learned the material in depth. Later on, in college, he excelled at essay tests, which really enabled him to display his in-depth knowledge of the subject. Eventually, his ability to learn a subject well and communicate it helped him make a successful living as a technical writer. What a valuable skill—and one he might not have developed had he been able to do better on multiple-choice tests!

To develop these skills, Jason had to keep running the race—to keep believing that he would eventually prevail. He had to develop perseverance—one of the personality traits most linked with success. It is also called *grit*.

Successful adults generally succeed by learning to manage the challenges of school—not by mastering every aspect of academics. Did Jason give up on study strategies just because he wasn't great at multiple choice? Or did Jason learn how to overcome his challenges and focus on his strengths rather than his weaknesses? Just like Jason, we must find ways to persevere no matter what challenges we face. These are the skills that translate directly to success in working life.

In our current culture, we frequently look for instant gratification. We want rewards *now*. But you are building a better *you*, and that takes time.

Think About It Everyone you admire—athlete, artist, activist, academic—has done something you thought was great. You know it took hard work. It took time. It took focus.

* Who do you admire?

* What have they achieved that you also want to achieve?

* Ever wonder how they did it?

* Do you think they were disorganized?

* Do you think they did it *quickly* or did it *right*?

They worked hard, sometimes for years, and definitely learned to overcome obstacles. And you know what? Because of your ADHD, you can become *great* at overcoming obstacles. You know you have to work hard, because many aspects of school haven't been easy for you. All the downsides of difficulties in school? Those are huge upsides.

When you think about your dreams and achieving your goals, remember that it is going to take hard work. But you *can* work hard. ADHD has made sure of that!

ADHD as Your Superpower

Several times we've mentioned that having ADHD has benefits. We've been pointing out that ADHD can make you work harder, because focusing doesn't come easily. But ADDYTeens can find many ways to make ADHD work *for you*. For example, creativity. Many ADDYTeens are very creative, connecting different aspects of the world in new and different ways. Humor: some ADDYTeens can be particularly outgoing and funny in part because of their ADHD.

Daring: you can think of daring as the "yes I can" benefit of ADHD. Being too cautious can be safe, but some impulsiveness can help you take risks—and to pursue great new ventures, you need this "yes I can" benefit. If you overthink your next move, then sometimes you wind up not doing anything. Being daring can help you start an enterprise that can bring you joy and security *and* move the world in new and different directions.

Thinking quickly: in sports, ADHD can be a benefit. It allows you to quickly assess a situation and make a plan without worrying over the consequences. It often leads to quicker reaction times. ADHD definitely allows you to concentrate in short, intense bursts of energy, which feels great to many ADDYTeens. If the sport absorbs your focus in the moment, you do not get distracted, while your ability to look around at many moving parts allows you to see the whole field. (Did you know that Michael Jordan was diagnosed with ADHD? That probably helped him track the movement of everybody on the court; he couldn't have done what he did if he just focused on his defender.) Without "yes I can," doing moves in gymnastics or X Games would be impossible!

For me, school was really difficult. My ADHD made it challenging to focus, remember what the teacher said in class lectures, or synthesize a quick class reading. But ADHD helped me see the world differently, and it gave me confidence to try things differently. Writing this book has not been easy. None of my friends has written a book! None of my friends collaborates with medical specialists like Dr. Sarah. I am successful because of my ADHD, not in spite of it.

There are many famous chefs with ADHD, such as Jamie Oliver. He never particularly excelled in school. The standard model of learning didn't quite work for him the way it works for others. Some way or other, experts like Chef Oliver have found their passion in the kitchen and made it their goal to create food masterpieces and become an executive leader in the kitchen. And because cooking takes concentration—tablespoons versus teaspoons matters—they felt successful when they managed to do it. The "yes I can" turns an ordinary cook into a restaurant owner or TV celebrity chef.

Just remember, ADHD can really help you in life, but it always needs to be managed to turn difficult experiences to your ultimate advantage.

chapter 2

Self-Care

Serious athletes know that their body is an amazing high-performance machine. What you put into your body and how you take care of your body impact your performance, just as a machine that receives regular lubrication and maintenance will do its best work. Your body can go and go and go, but it's up to you to make sure your body and mind can work to the best of their ability.

When we think of winning with ADHD, taking care of the body is a crucial factor to consider. When we don't eat right, fail to regularly move our bodies around, or don't get enough sleep, our bodies feel it! When we don't eat well, our body must strain to produce the energy we need. We often get cranky, irritable, and tired. Have you heard the term *hangry*—hungry and angry? We turn into hangry monsters when we don't take in good nutrition.

ADHD makes many of us quick to anger anyway, and skipping meals can exacerbate this. When you are hangry, it's hard to settle down and focus. This chapter is about taking care of your machine, making sure you know how to keep your body healthy so you can perform at your best—academically, socially, and personally.

Feeding Your Machine: Eating Right

Your brain is, pound for pound, the most metabolically active part of your body. So it needs to be fed! When you have that low-energy feeling, you tend to think in a less focused way. Nutritious foods—high in protein, healthy fat, and complex carbohydrates—tend to give you more steady energy during the whole day, and that helps you focus. Yes, junk foods high in refined sugar give you a quick burst of energy, but they are often followed by a "crash," meaning a low-energy feeling.

Many of us run around all day from morning until night. Sometimes it seems that we never really get a chance to relax and decompress. However, that is never an excuse to skip a meal, especially breakfast, even if you are running late or disorganized!

Teens usually give one of two usual explanations for not eating breakfast: (1) I don't have time, and (2) I'm not hungry. In the first case, *make* the time! It can be a five-minute meal. In the second case, eat anyway; don't wait until you are hungry.

For those who take medicine for our ADHD, eating healthy and consistently can be a little challenging. Some medications for ADHD, specifically the stimulant forms, can curb your appetite for lunch. If you are taking those kinds of medications, it's doubly important to eat a good breakfast.

Some ADDYTeens (often boys) are concerned about not gaining enough weight on the stimulant medications; others (often girls) tend to be happier with the possibility of appetite suppression. But listen up, all of you ADDYTeens: you *all* get cranky and have a harder time focusing when you don't eat right.

For me, a change in appetite came as a surprise. I was used to eating three or four times a day, but with my medicine, I would eat breakfast and dinner with rarely anything in between. This was a challenge, because I was in school for eight hours a day, and school required me to focus, produce good work, and, well, stay awake. I found it helpful to pack nutritious snacks like nuts, fruit, or a sandwich that I could eat on the go when I felt myself losing steam in the middle of the day and also during after-school activities.

Take Action Studies have shown benefits in academic performance when you eat breakfast before school. Seems like an easy way to boost your performance! If you feel like you don't have enough time for breakfast in the morning, consider the following quick options:

* Hard-boiled eggs made the day before and kept in the fridge

* Omelet

* Yogurt

* Cheese

* Oatmeal with nuts

* Protein bars in the car on the way to school

   Or think about some non-breakfast foods you may like:

* Peanut butter and jelly

* Sliced turkey

Packing small, quick snacks for when you are on the go during the day is a smart move too! Nuts, veggies, cheese, deli meat, and fresh or dried fruits are great choices.

Maintaining Your Machine: Exercising

Exercise is good for your brain, too! Exercise helps ADDYTeens focus. Some ADDYTeens are physically hyperactive—always wanting to move, fidget, and generally be active. Others are physically quite calm, but mentally inattentive. Exercise can help both types.

Dr. Sarah Says Exercise causes physical changes in the brain that lead to improved focus. When you exercise, there is an increase in certain proteins, such as brain-derived neurotrophic factor (BDNF), which are thought to help with learning, focus, and memory. Exercise also improves mood and reduces anxiety.

When you are physically tired from exercise, it's also easier to sit still for class. So even apart from all the cardio-vascular benefits, regular exercise directly benefits your brain and mood. I have seen some people get by without medications by exercising twice a day—commonly before school and before homework.

But exercise does not mean a walk around the block. Exercise should boost your heart rate and breathing and make you sweat.

Exercise doesn't have to be *work*. It can be a fun activity that you look forward to. It can be biking in a beautiful area, Frisbee with friends, jogging on the beach. If you are doing a sport you love after school, that's fantastic, but if you are not truly enjoying your team sport, don't feel compelled to continue—it can be a huge time commitment. To get the benefits, a workout doesn't have to be a three-hour team practice—a half hour to an hour is enough. (But be wary of team sports that lead to multiple concussions. Those sure don't help you focus.)

And there's more great news: if you make exercise a regular part of your life, you keep creating great blood flow to the brain and great chemicals in the brain, and you help ensure that you have a healthy, functioning brain throughout your life. You get only one brain. Take care of it.

Take Action   Need to exercise, but don't like running? What else can you do? Get creative! At home, try a trampoline or mini trampoline, or one of a million online boot camp-type videos. Get a pull-up bar. If you like to exercise with others but don't want to be on a traditional team, try fencing, boxing, racquetball/squash, dancing, Quidditch, tennis, rock climbing, or hiking in the woods!

Improving Your Machine: Sleep

You know what happens when we don't get enough sleep? We have a hard time concentrating and remembering things. ADDYTeens: you must avoid anything that makes it harder to concentrate, focus, and remember things. Seriously. Sleep = no-brainer.

ADDYTeens need eight to ten hours of sleep a night, on average. Yes, you may have friends who swear they only need five or six hours, but your friends are either sleep-deprived and fibbing about it or quite unusual in regard to their sleep needs. More likely you need about nine hours of sleep.

Dr. Sarah Says   Sleep is a crucial factor when trying to get your brain in an optimal state to focus. We all love sleep, but often we don't get enough. I have told this to many ADDYTteens, who respond, "I don't need that much sleep; I'm fine on just a few hours."

They may feel fine to themselves, but other people notice a difference. Also, studies show that your thinking is affected by even mild sleep deprivation, despite your feeling "fine." In other words, you may actually be performing worse than you think you are.

And if you need additional motivation, lack of sleep can cause or aggravate acne. Yuck!

It's important to get not only enough hours of sleep but also good-quality sleep. (See the Take Action coming up for tips.) If you are getting enough hours of sleep but still feel tired, tell a parent or doctor. Some ADDYTeens have problems breathing at night (sleep apnea) or mood issues (anxiety or depression) that can interfere with sleep quality. Unfortunately, ADDYTeens seem to be at a higher risk of sleep issues than teens without ADHD.

It's okay to relax in bed with a book, some music, or a TV show, but you need to make time for enough sleep for your mind to be fresh and ready to go the next morning. If you have to cut out anything, don't make it your sleep.

If you aren't getting enough, aim to at least increase the amount you're getting. If you're getting six hours, aim for six and a half or seven. Even that little increase can help. It can seem incredibly hard to get a whole two hours more of sleep, and many ADDYTeens don't even want to try. If you're used to going to bed at midnight and then suddenly go to bed at 10 p.m., it may be hard to power down. It's better to gradually move to an earlier bedtime.

Even without outside disturbances, there are a number of physical conditions that could interfere with your sleep quality to some degree, and you might not realize you have them. Some people have many mini-awakenings per hour and don't even know it. This is called sleep apnea. If you snore (you may not hear it, but your family does!), that is one sign that you might have sleep apnea (although many snorers don't have apnea). Being physically restless while sleeping can also wake you up.

Take Action

* Make sleep a priority. Realize it will be good for you to get more sleep, and try to plan your schedule to allow for it.

* No electronics at least one hour before bed (if possible) and certainly no electronics in the bed at night. Turn the phone *off*.

* Keep room lights low (40 watts or less) in the one to two hours before bedtime. First thing in the morning, expose your face to sunlight. This helps establish your circadian (daily) rhythm.

* Reserve your bedroom for sleeping, as much as possible. Try to do homework or other activities in another room. That way, when you walk into your bedroom your body is ready for sleep.

* Keep your room quiet and dark. Blackout curtains or shades help; so does covering all light sources (such as monitor lights and digital clocks) with black tape. Earplugs can really help (though they take a bit of getting used to).

* Try to keep about the same schedule every day. It is tempting to sleep in on the weekend, but that can make it very hard to get to sleep later, which throws your whole schedule off.

* Keep naps short. If they are too long, it also makes it hard to sleep that night.

Dealing with Stress

Home is often where we freak out and feel like we have too much to do. Then it's hard to focus on getting one thing done, and that puts most of us in a bad mood, so even the smallest conversation with parents or friends may set us off!

ADDYTeens often tell us how stressed out they are. It's probably the biggest emotional issue they face. Unfortunately, stress can lead to significant depression and anxiety for both ADDYTeen boys and girls. Juggling tough classes is a full-time job in itself; sport or robotic team commitments could add an extra fifteen hours per week at least. Downtime? That's hard to squeeze in.

How do we fix this? First, working on procrastination and using our time wisely should help. The next chapter provides a lot of coaching on managing time and getting organized. You may hate this idea, but using your time wisely and being organized means less stress, not more.

Managing your ADHD greatly reduces stress. We will show you how.

Work Hard, Play Hard

Managing your ADHD is all about balancing your mind and your body. This means working hard and letting yourself rest and recuperate on your time off. When you work, work hard. Period. When you play, play hard! Do one, then the other. Be sure to have *off* times as well as *on* times—they are both important!

At school and in many other situations (such as a music lesson), focusing and working hard is required. Whether it is reading, taking notes, or turning your homework in on time, you spend a lot of brainpower getting these tasks done. When you work, you need to make sure that you're in an environment that fosters concentration and focus.

It's important to give yourself the time you need to regain your energy and strength. We can't work all the time, right? We need to balance work time and play time, to keep ourselves happy and ready for the next day. This means going out and enjoying the sun, our friends, and our family! Don't feel guilty about taking breaks; without them, great work is impossible.

However, make break time something you can stop. If you *love* a particular computer game, and once you start you can't stop playing it, that is a bad break activity. However, if you work diligently for an hour, maybe then taking the time to play your favorite video game is more a reward than an excuse to procrastinate. Physical activities, such as a set of push-ups or sit-ups or a walk around the block, can also be good breaks. And of course, your breaks should be much shorter than your work time.

Let's Hear from ADDYTeens

Kevin, sixteen, loved to play video games. He could spend hours on his console, not noticing any time had gone by, even forgetting to eat or drink. Not surprisingly, his grades suffered, and his weight ballooned as he spent all his free time sitting in front of the screen. He kept telling his parents and himself that he needed gaming to "relax and have fun." When he saw Dr. Sarah, they added up all the hours that he spent playing video games each week: about five hours every weekday and closer to eight each weekend day. A grand total of 41 hours per week, 177 hours per month, and 2,132 hours per year! (Dr. Sarah notes that these hours are not unusual among ADDYTeens she treats.) And Kevin could not stop thinking about his games. His parents were very upset and constantly asking him to stop playing. Kevin and Dr. Sarah disagreed about the right number of hours to spend on video games, but he agreed to play in big chunks only on weekends, but not Monday through Thursday. His parents agreed to let him play on weekends without harassing him. During the weeks his breaks were for physical activities. He started with jumping on the trampoline, then going on short runs and then longer runs. Kevin still played a lot of video games, but he enjoyed playing them more when he had free rein to do so. Plus, as his weight normalized, he got into fantastic shape, and he enjoyed feeling slimmer, lighter, and stronger.

Sometimes you can work in big chunks of time. Other times the work period will be shorter. Either way, when you work, give it your full focus. Working with minimal energy can lead to silly mistakes and a poor-quality completed assignment. Similarly, when you decide to hang out with friends or engage in some good old self-care, make sure you're not worrying about uncompleted tasks. It's all about managing your ADHD—which we're going to tackle in the next chapter.

chapter 3

Managing Your ADHD

Listen up, ADDYTeens. If you want to win with ADHD; if you want to achieve your goals; if you want to be a good friend, a good kid, a good student, a good worker—you need to learn how to manage your life. Real talk: nothing in life is free! This is your life; you need to decide how you want to live it. Mom can't fix this; Dad can't fix this. You must put in effort to achieve any goal, big or small. Joining a select soccer team, getting a scholarship, and graduating from high school all require effort. What do you want to do?

- Your coach in soccer or baseball can teach you—but you play.

- Your music or drama instructor can teach you—but you play.

We are going to teach you here too—and give you Plays to practice, just like you get in soccer, baseball, band practice, and piano lessons.

So in this chapter we will coach you in how to get organized and stay organized. Heads up! We said *managing* your ADHD.

Go ahead, look up the word *managing* in the dictionary; here is what you will find:

- To be in charge of

- To lead

- To supervise

- To succeed

- To organize

- To cope

Think of how a baseball manager coaches a team. There are many different factors to consider when coaching a team: becoming aware of other players' emotions about their performance, using positive communication, and collaborating with the rest of the team. These skills are not just for baseball coaching—they're also for our daily activities. We all need these skills to perform our best in school, in sports, with family, and in life!

This book is about winning with ADHD, and to win, you need to learn how to manage—to lead, be in charge, supervise, achieve your goals, cope, and thrive.

We like to break a big challenge down into smaller ones; it's easier to manage that way. So we are going to break down the challenge of learning how to manage into five sections:

- Getting Organized

- Managing Your Time

- Managing Your Stuff

- Managing Your Emotions

- Speaking Up for Yourself

Getting Organized

ADDYTeens all face some common challenges—and one of them is getting organized. Yeah, yeah, you have heard this before. You hear it from parents, coaches, friends, and teachers—they all say, "Get organized!"

ADDYTeens are very prone to being disorganized. And when ADDYTeens are not interested in something, it's really much harder for them to do it. We know most of you are just not interested in being organized.

OK, real talk. Just hearing the word *organization* freaks me out a little. Some people are naturally organized. I am not. Seriously, when I was growing up my room was so messy it was like a tornado hit it. To be organized basically meant I had to be on top of my game.

How does being organized benefit you? Check it out:

- Athletes know when their practices and games are; where their uniforms are (and they are clean); where their bags, cleats; and pads are, and so much more.

- Rappers keep their lyric ideas and poems in journals or books and spend a lot of time every day practicing so they seem natural.

- Actors keep up with rehearsals, learn their lines, and prepare to work with their fellow actors to present their performances.

Sounds like a lot of work for any one person, right? It is. But it's not just one's person's work. Being organized benefits not just the player, but also the whole team! Not just the actor, but also the entire cast. Can you imagine if the star quarterback on the football team forgot his pads and cleats? Or showed up two hours late to his big game? He and his whole team would be in trouble. Do you think LeBron or Kobe, Manning or Brady, Eminem or Jay-Z became so accomplished by being disorganized? The same goes for us.

OK, first things first. What does it mean to be organized? Go ahead, look up the word *organize* in the dictionary; you'll find "To structure; to plan; to prepare." If you are one of the 5 percent of ADDYTeens who are already organized, then we suggest you read some of the Plays in this chapter for tips on how to make yourself even more effective at it. For the 95 percent who are not, let's agree on some basics:

1. Being organized is about saving time.

2. ADDYTeens need more time—to do homework, to study, to take tests, to do chores.

3. If you save time, you get more done, you have more fun, you feel more in control.

4. Getting more done, having more fun, and feeling more in control—*makes you happier!*

5. Getting more done is winning!

6. Being in control is winning!

7. Having more fun is winning!

Getting and staying organized is *huge* for ADDYTeens. It's simple, people! Just think about it.

- You get to places on time.

- You get to places with the things you need (lunch, phone, papers).

- You know what is coming up and can schedule time to prepare—for example, for tests. It's easier to do well on a test if you know you are going to be taking it!

- You look organized and appear more responsible to other people.

Heads up, ADDYTeens! Read that last one again! *You look organized and appear more responsible to other people.* This is a *big one.* You don't live alone in this world. Other people judge you:

- Your parents notice when you are trying your best— and when you are not.

- Your friends like it when you show up—and don't when you flake out.

- Teachers grade you, in part, on your effort and ability to turn in work on time.

- Adults decide whether to hire you (for a babysitting job, for example) in part based on whether you seem responsible.

Why is being disorganized a problem?

Can you imagine forgetting a huge school project on the day it's due, leaving your field trip ticket on the dining table, or forgetting to bring your lunch to school? I can. I've done it many times. And being disorganized contributes to our stress! Think about it. Remember crying, complaining you have no free time, that your homework takes too long, that you can't do your chores?

When you are disorganized...

- You spend time looking for things.

- You lose things.

- You show up to class or practice without the things you need.

- You are not prepared for tests.

- You are not prepared in class.

- You forget to show up for family and friends.

- Then you get even more stressed about all of this.

- And you get stressed about making your family and friends angry—when you did not mean to and in fact feel bad about.

Sure, getting organized is a pain, but it's better than the stress of being disorganized!

Now, are you motivated to get organized? We will show you how.

Managing Your Time

Remember elementary school? Life was so simple. You just showed up to class with your lunch—easy. Most of the work you did was in class. Very little homework, very few projects, very few deadlines.

But when you enter middle school, move on to high school, and then go to college, life changes a lot—especially for ADDYTeens. You must get organized and keep track of many types of homework, projects, and deadlines.

Which is easier: to remember twenty different items you need to take care of, or to remember just one rule? That rule is to *write it down*. Calendars, to-do lists, and phone reminders can help you keep yourself and your time organized.

How do you manage your time now? Where do you write down your schedule of tasks, homework, chores, practice times, project deadlines, dates with friends, parties, games, piano lessons? Yep—your calendar!! We recommend getting a planner—a notebook with daily and weekly calendars—very handy! We also recommend getting a big monthly calendar for home, where you and your family can see what you have to do and when.

Before I got organized, staying on track with my schedule and activities seemed like a joke. It wasn't my fault I couldn't remember when my homework was due or when my next soccer game was. This pattern not only made me look bad in front of my class, my friends, and my crush, but it also kept me behind. How embarrassing. I got sick of it, and I changed.

I never used a planner in elementary school, but since I was in middle school when I learned about my ADHD, I thought maybe it was worth a try. My peers would use their planner to write down their homework assignment and due date and even noted which class lesson matched up with the homework of that day. They also put in the time and location of their sports practice and who ran carpool that day. I just looked at the board to remember my homework...but that didn't end up so well. I got a planner.

The Foundational Play Managing Your Time is great for any project, from a test or paper to a party you plan to throw for your friends. I like to use one color for each activity or theme I am writing about—purple for homework, green for soccer practice and games, orange for chores around the house, and blue for hangouts with my friends.

Pick your favorite colors for your chores and for your hobbies. Time is a valuable resource; use it wisely. Think about this: It's Sunday night, and you have a whole week ahead of you. Basketball practice Monday, Wednesday, and Thursday; homework for at least three hours every weeknight, and chores you have to keep up with for the week. Not to mention upcoming projects! Managing your time is an essential skill.

I spent a lot more time doing any particular assignment than any one of my friends did. When I was fifteen or sixteen, it was a *total drag*! Now that I am in college, it's the same; I still need more time. However, now I know how to manage my time, manage my stress, and perform better in class, because I stay organized.

Many of my college friends never learned how to stay organized, and many have failed out, or have to do all-nighters just to catch up before finals. They get C's instead of B's and A's.

I never have to do all-nighters, I never cram for finals—because I chip away at my work in small segments, not all at once. I frequently get much better grades than most of my friends, and I have less stress than I used to. Do some of my friends get by without working hard in class or staying organized? Sure, a few do. I can't.

Foundational Play: Managing Your Time

1. Schedule your deadlines.

    Why: To make sure you are prepared to win!

    How: Create a calendar entry for the day and time that each project has to be ready or finished.

2. List required tasks.

    Why: To break down big projects into smaller, more manageable tasks.

    How: Number each task, and generously estimate the hours required.

3. Plan your work.

    Why: To be prepared and ready for each deadline!

    How: On your calendar, mark one-hour blocks of time for each task. If you've allocated three hours for one task, mark three one-hour blocks on the days leading up to your deadline.

4. Work your plan—before school.

   Why: To make sure you are ready for the day and don't forget anything.

   How: After breakfast at home, check what work or materials you need to bring to class or to any after-school activity—lunch, wallet, keys, phone—and make sure you bring them.

5. Work your plan—during school.

   Why: To update your calendar with new assignments and make sure you plan for fun only when not busy with other tasks.

   How: In class, add new assignments and deadlines; ask all about the assignments and write detailed notes in your planner.

6. Work your plan—after school.

   Why: To get your work done *right*.

   How: Do the work you listed in your calendar. Simple!

7. Work your plan—before bed.

   Why: To prepare for the next day.

   How: Organize your stuff—homework, materials, backpack—for the next day for less stress in the morning.

8. Manage your plan.

   Why: To adjust your schedule when a task needs more or less time.

   How: In this check step, see if you have allocated too much or too little time for a task. Add more thirty-minute slots if needed. Fill cleared time slots with another task.

Quick Summary:

Step 1: Schedule Your Deadlines

Step 2: List Required Tasks

Step 3: Plan Your Work.

Step 4: Work Your Plan Before School

Step 5: Work Your Plan During School

Step 6: Work Your Plan After School

Step 7: Work Your Plan Before Bed

Step 8: Manage Your Plan

Set Play: Practice Drill!

OK, now let's apply this to a real-life example, then you'll repeat this on your own with your own tasks. Imagine it's Friday, lunchtime. You have three more classes and then you are off for the weekend. Woo-hoo! You have a plan to hang out with your friends after school! But hold up; you have three more classes:

1 p.m. in science class, your teacher says you have a test the following Wednesday, covering chapter 4 in your textbook.

2 p.m. in English, your teacher wants you to be ready Monday to discuss *To Kill a Mockingbird*, which you have been reading all week.

3 p.m. in Spanish, you are told there will be a quiz next Tuesday on ten new verb conjugations.

With this information, use your planner to manage your time so you are prepared and meet all three deadlines. Check out steps 4 through 8 to get started!

Managing Your Stuff

Do you cook dinner in the bathroom? Do you shower in the kitchen? Uhhh…no.

There is a place for all the things and activities in a home, and you are responsible for your own environment. ADDYTeens, heads up! Distraction is our middle name—every one of us finds distraction a problem. What can you do about it?

This section is about learning how to manage your environment, so you avoid distractions, which can hinder us in attending to and completing our tasks. Everything takes longer when you're distracted—and who wants to spend a minute longer on homework than they have to? Not us. Also, when you get distracted doing something, not only does it take longer, but you also start to think that everyone else is better than you at doing that activity because they finish it faster. That leads to *What's wrong with me?* which then leads to *Why even bother starting?*

Distractions are natural and inevitable, and dealing with them takes effort, but it is not impossible.

What is distracting? Anything that makes it harder to focus and stay on task. This depends on where we are, who we're with, and what we're doing. At home, it may be social media and our phone. At school, it may be our friends or even a bird flying by. With friends, it may be a cute boy or girl walking by. So, what's the problem?

- Distractions generate mistakes.

- Mistakes add to your stress.

- Distractions waste time.

- Time is your most valuable resource.

- You have to learn to use your time wisely, so removing distractions is key.

You are probably a lot smarter than your tests or grades show—why? When you get distracted, you make more mistakes.

When trying to deal with your distractions, look first to your environment. Many events—like school, team practice, a leadership or yearbook meeting—require you to sit still and concentrate, for your sake and the sake of your peers. Giving your peers and teammates active participation and attention is not only respectful but also a great skill to learn for working in groups.

Dr. Sarah Says The key to thriving and winning with ADHD is moving from an unfocused, distracted state to a focused state. To do this, you want to do the things that make you more focused, not less.

* Trying to work in a noisy, messy room? That leads to less focus.

* Trying to work with your phone beeping next to you? That leads to less focus.

* Sitting up straight at a clean desk, where you look and feel like a good student? That leads to more focus.

Think about where you did your homework yesterday. Were you distracted? By what?

Think about your room this morning. Was it neat or messy? Does stuff lying around help you focus?

Life gets easier when you get organized. You can easily find things. You spend less time looking for things. You have what you need, when you need it—and it's not all crumpled up.

But again, getting organized is often a challenge for ADDYTeens. As an ADDYTeen, you may sprint past the menial tasks of organizing your papers in your rush to "just do things." Hello: you just make bigger messes and lose more of your stuff. As a consequence, you may miss the "easy credit points" of school. You may do all the work, but then lose it. Since you don't turn it in, you don't get credit. Then, for partial credit you redo the assignment for less credit (read: "twice the work for less reward"). That is frustrating—for you, your teacher, your parents, and others watching you.

Yes, sometimes you do turn in your work and your *teacher* loses it—but that's pretty rare. Most teachers have systems in place to ensure that they collect, grade, and hand back assignments. And that is what you need also—a system.

The first step to managing your stuff in school is learning how to organize your backpack! After that, how you do it is up to you. We'll give you a few guidelines, then you can figure out a system that suits you.

Take Action

* Spend a couple of minutes every day throwing out junk you don't need. You can do this when you empty your lunch box or pack up your backpack at the end of the evening.

* Pack up your backpack in the evening when you have time, rather than in the morning when you are in a frantic rush and more likely to just jam things in.

* Keep your organization system simple. Color-coding and filing homework alphabetically may not be realistic for you—or necessary. You can file by subject, or put all homework you'll be completing in one folder and all completed homework in another.

* Refine your system as you go along. What you thought might be a good idea at the start of the school year may not actually work for the idiosyncrasies of a particular class.

ADDYTeens, in this section we will work on the Foundational Play Managing Your Work Area. The goal is to help you pick the right environment to work in at home and stay on track. Step by step, you can do it.

Foundational Play: Managing Your Work Area

1. Pick the right location.

    Why: To make a special place to study or succeed at homework.

    How: At home, pick a quiet space where you can close the door. At the library, pick a quiet desk away from your friends.

2. Get prepared.

    Why: To use your time wisely, making sure you have the necessary materials.

    How: Once you sit down to work, you'll need to stay seated and focus. To prepare, neatly organize your planner, calendar, computer, notebooks, calculator, syllabus, books, and past assignments.

3. Remove distractions.

    Why: To help you focus.

    How: Bring in snacks and water so you don't have to get up for them. Manage your electronics (see the following section). Remove anything on your desk or table that isn't part of your study or homework. Put a "Studying: Do Not Disturb" sign on the outside of the door and close it. Close the windows too.

4. Keep your space clean.

    Why: To earn your family's respect for your space, by showing respect for it yourself.

    How: After studying, clean up. Remove all trash, glasses, and plates that held drinks and snacks. Store past assignments in the class folder and put it in your backpack.

5. Organize your backpack.

    Why: To make sure you have your completed work in your backpack for class the next day.

    How: Pack up your backpack when you are calm. You are more likely to take the time to get organized when you pack the night before, rather than during a hectic morning.

Bottom line: make sure your environment leads to more focus, not less. Organize and keep your space clean—not for your parents, but for yourself.

Managing Your Electronics

ADDYTeens, you need to turn off your phone more than you might like to. Get used to it. Facebook, Instagram, Twitter, messaging—none of this gets you into college, gets you onto the varsity squad, gets you a job.

You have heard your parents say this—or scream it at you: when you need to study and do homework, turn off your electronics and *keep them off*! Electronics are designed by teams of scientists to grab your attention and keep it there. It's you against a team of neuropsychologists. If you play their game, they are going to win. So stay out of it.

Remember Control the Controllables in the introduction? This is one of the big ones. Remember when we talked about helping yourself to focus naturally? Do the things that help you focus, and avoid the things that get you distracted.

Yes, we know that you *need* electronics to interface with school assignments—for some, you must watch YouTube videos or check online to see what is due. But there are apps that help you manage how long you spend on certain sites, or block ones you don't need. Some will automatically close windows for you to lessen distractions. (See my website, www.addyteen.com, for a list of online resources.)

Dr. Sarah Says Some teens feel that music helps them concentrate. Studies indicate that some kinds of music may do that, including music without much variation in tones or volume, and also purely instrumental music. Songs that you can sing along to tend to be more distracting than most teens think. If you want to listen to music, do it before you study to make you more happy and relaxed—then turn it off!

Managing Your Emotions

Sure, we get upset and have meltdowns. Everyone does. But how do we cope emotionally?

Emotions need to be managed, or they will manage you. Don't misunderstand: feeling your emotions and listening to your body is important. However, knowing how and when to defuse your emotions and energy when you're worked up is equally if not more important. Getting a grip on your emotions is easier said than done. When you're all worked up in the moment, regulating your emotions can seem impossible.

In chapter 1 we noted that some ADDYTeens are impulsive, acting without first thinking or planning. Yep, we can be more impulsive than those without ADHD. That means that we too frequently respond to situations quickly—with anger, with feeling overwhelmed, with anxiety—instead of slowing down and thinking and reasoning through a situation. Our emotions can get in the way of being able to deal with a situation and focusing on the issues we need to resolve. So, for example, some ADDYTeens get irritated very easily, and instead of rationally being able to accept help, they lash out. Personally, I get overwhelmed when there seems to be too much to do, and then sometimes I panic and feel unable to start addressing my challenges. We ADDYTeens need to manage these emotions.

Over the years I have found it helpful to follow three easy steps: Acknowledge, Identify, Defuse (easy to remember as "AID").

1. **Acknowledge:** Notice *how and when* you start getting upset. Where are you? Who are you with? What factors triggered you to feel this way? Are you hungry? Tired? Then, when a similar situation arises and people say you are irritable, you know they may be right. You can also take some steps to calm yourself down even before you erupt.

2. **Identify:** Pay attention to exactly *what* you are feeling. It is important to name and label your emotions to help you sort them. Since we often feel many emotions at the same time, we may unintentionally group them together. But anger, fear, shame, and distress are each distinct. Even if you don't know exactly what to call your emotions, saying that you're feeling "funky" or "pissy" is fine too. Name your emotions whatever you like.

3. **Defuse:** This means "prevent from exploding." Once you've identified *what factors* contribute to your feelings, and also *what* you feel, focus on what you can control, and work to defuse your emotions. If they were triggered by being hungry, eat something. If you are tired, take a break, walk around the block, listen to music. If there is a person who regularly really upsets you, ask yourself why that is. Are they in the wrong? Or are they saying something that may be hitting too close to home?

Create a moment of silence in which you can review the situation, your actions, and the actions of others. Remember, too, that though it may be easier for you to point the finger and blame someone else, you must also review your own actions and behavior in order to move forward in a healthy way.

> **Dr. Sarah Says** Think of your brain as having two parts: an emotional part and a rational, "thinking" part. Grace's strategies work because they calm down the angry, emotional part of the brain while trying to empower the rational part. Think of these two parts of the brain as having a tug-of-war inside your head. Throw your weight behind the rational side.

Let's put AID to work in your life. Using the next Foundational Play will help you manage your emotions and reduce the stress in your life.

Foundational Play: Regulating Your Emotions

1. Acknowledge something is wrong.

   Why: To learn to get in touch with your feelings.

   How: When you're upset and don't know what is bothering you, take a time-out and just acknowledge that something is off.

2. Identify the feeling.

   Why: To help you manage specific emotions.

   How: Identify and label the different emotions you are feeling rather than grouping them as one bad feeling. Give each your own unique word. My favorites are "funky," "pissy," and "edgy."

3. Detect the triggers.

   Why: To understand what caused your emotions.

   If a similar situation happens again, you'll be better able to recognize potential emotions and control them more easily.

   How: Relax and consider what made you feel so emotional. Link how you feel to recent situations.

4. Defuse—get into the moment.

   Why: To gain control by being here and now.

   How: Focus on only what you can control in the moment, not in the past or future. Don't waste time and energy on what you can't control.

5. Consider the situation.

   Why: To step back and see the big picture.

   How: Think about the entire situation. Are you upset with yourself or someone else? Consider both sides—yours and theirs.

6. Express your emotions.

Why: To get your deeply buried emotions out so you can manage them.

How: Express your emotions in a healthy and safe way, then step back and take some time for yourself.

- Walk around the block.

- Listen to some music.

- Take a shower.

- Take a moment and collect your thoughts.

- Count back from ten to one.

- Don't insist on having the last word.

- Step out of the room and give yourself space.

7. Revisit and redo.

Why: To resolve the issue that triggered the emotion.

How: Return to the situation when you are calm and have collected yourself. Speak actively:

I feel _____ when you tell me _____.

_____ makes me feel _____.

I will do _____ better next time we talk

about _____.

> **Dr. Sarah Says**   Many people with ADHD easily become anxious. Your brain may be seeing a lot of things that need doing yet be unable to complete enough tasks to feel like you are making a dent in them. Think of the feeling you get when you come back from vacation and have so many things crying out for you to do, all at once. People become anxious when they think about things that need doing in the future. People are not anxious about the present. Focus on the present moment.

Speaking Up for Yourself

I think speaking up for yourself is the most important skill ADDYTeens need to master. It's like a free throw in basketball— you have the court to yourself, no one is blocking you, and you have plenty of time to prepare. For ADDYTeens, learning to speak up for what you need is especially important because often we need a little extra support. If you're hesitant to ask for help because everyone else seems to be doing fine, consider this: What if a soccer player needed help with their defense but was too afraid to tell their coach, because the rest of the team didn't need help? Even if the rest of the team doesn't need help, shouldn't the one player still speak up for what they need? Absolutely.

Just like this soccer player, we all have strengths and weaknesses. What may seem challenging to us—say, taking notes and listening to a teacher's lecture at the same time—may not be challenging for others. But that doesn't mean we shouldn't speak up for ourselves and ask for help. This not only helps us succeed but also reflects our engagement and proactivity.

Speaking up for yourself to your teacher, coach, parents, or friends is the only way you'll get what you need from others in life. No one can read minds; you need to speak up (that is, advocate) for yourself. Bonus: this helps others understand your strengths and weaknesses too!

Advocating for myself is a skill I learned after I got diagnosed with ADHD. I learned to speak up about many things I needed help with, for example, politely asking someone to turn their music down while I was studying, or asking my teacher for notes before class lecture starts.

We've been focused on managing your time mainly as it relates to school; in the next chapter, we'll tackle managing your ADHD at home.

chapter 4

ADHD at Home

ADDYTeens, having ADHD is not just about school, tests, and grades (chapter 5 will focus on that part of your life). Being an ADHD thinker affects your life at home too. And these are issues that don't just go away when you shut your bedroom door! This chapter is about managing your ADHD at home—where chores await, procrastination lurks, and parents are bugging you!

Managing Responsibilities

Oh, man—any teen knows that things can get pretty chaotic around the house. For ADDYTeens, the combination of school responsibilities plus the tasks, chores, and other family obligations at home can quickly become overwhelming and hard to manage.

At home, some parents give teens a lot to do. Have you heard the philosophy, "Doing work builds character"? Dang! We already have a lot to do! We have school, band rehearsal, and soccer practice during weekdays, and math problems, chapters to read, dogs to walk, and our room to clean nights and weekends. Our parents give us stuff to do. Our coaches and music teachers give us stuff to do. The directors of the plays we're in give us stuff to do. The list goes on and on.

Plus, at home we may have a lot of chores to do beyond just cleaning our own room. We may have younger siblings to babysit, a dishwasher to empty, rugs to vacuum, trash to take out.

How can you make your life at home less chaotic and stressful? Start by thinking about your family like a team and yourself as a player on that team. Each team member has their own responsibilities on the field. In soccer, the goalie, the defense, the midfielders, and the strikers each have individual training for their position, but each player makes a team unit. Whether you're setting the screen or taking the game-winning shot, you don't want to let your team down, do you? Families are no different.

Many ADDYTeens find it easier to manage at school or work than to manage at home. Sometimes that creates confusion, especially for parents. Sometimes it creates friction. If you can get things done in one situation, they reason, why can't you do that at home? So you get accused of not wanting to, or being lazy!

But school and home are very different. School is highly structured; home is much more free-form. Yeah, we might have to take out the trash on a particular day, but *when* on that particular day? We have some leeway. We might have to clean our room, but maybe there is no agreement on *how* clean, or when the room gets *how* cluttered. And so on.

Face it: doing tasks at home is different from doing tasks at school.

- At school, there is the structure of class schedules and classrooms.

- We have homework clearly marked for a certain date.

- We take tests at very specific dates and times.

- Our classes start and end at the same time.

- Roles are clearly defined: you are a student; she or he is a teacher.

Remember, ADHD is how you think, and structure leads to focus. When you go to school, the bell rings, and that automatically sends *math class, where you are doing math* to the forefront of your brain. If you don't go, you are standing in the halls by yourself, feeling ridiculous. If you go to math and don't do math (while seeing everyone around you doing math) that also is pretty weird. But at home? It's likely that most of the time, everyone is doing their own thing whenever.

Even if you set an alarm to unload the dishwasher, nothing really prevents you from lapsing into an Instagram coma right after you turn off the alarm. So now we are going to coach you on getting focused in situations with less structure!

Growing up with ADHD is challenging, but I have a great team. My mom and dad really support me and don't compare me to other kids who don't have learning issues. I am lucky, but that does not mean my home was anything less than a battlefield much of the time. I did a lot of screaming and yelling when my parents held me accountable for mistakes that my lack of organization made worse. Being disorganized created problems for me, and it put me in conflict with those I loved, who were trying to help me. My bad! I had to fix that—and you can too.

OK, let's suit up. Chores at home are your responsibility. Accepting our responsibilities is the first step to doing them.

Dr. Sarah sees some ADDYTeens who accept their responsibilities more than others. Some feel it's fine to have to do some of the chores around the house or to attend a family event. Others are stressed with how much work they have at school and feel they don't have any remaining time or energy to contribute.

When you don't accept your responsibilities, it's harder for you to make yourself do them. At basketball, swimming, or soccer practice, you do endless drills—just like chores—but your whole team is doing them. Your family is your team; you need to support your team. Your whole family does chores, so you have to also.

Sometimes you need to ask for a pass, like when you are injured and can't practice your drills. If you do this all the time, your coach will become pissed. Same at home. If you feel that you can't accept your assigned chores, instead of just not doing them, talk to your family and see if there is a different way you can contribute. Is taking out the trash something you hate? Maybe you can try weeding the garden instead. But learning to do your fair share, whatever that is in your house, is an important part of growing up. Plus, you need to get used to doing tasks you don't necessarily enjoy. Hello! That's life.

Sure, getting all your responsibilities completed can be a lot to manage, but using tools like a big calendar or a smartphone can not only help you stay organized at home but also remind and encourage you to start and complete your work.

Our approach is to treat obligations at home just like obligations at school. Let's take the Foundational Play Managing Your Time in chapter 3 and apply it to Managing Responsibilities at Home.

Set Play: Managing Responsibilities at Home

1. Schedule your deadlines.

   Why: To make sure you complete your chores as needed by your home team (your family).

   How: Create a calendar entry for each chore on the date and time you're supposed to be ready or finished.

2. List required tasks.

   Why: To break down big projects into smaller tasks, which are easier to handle.

   How: Number each task and estimate—generously—the hours required.

3. Plan your work.

   Why: To be prepared and ready for each deadline!

   How: On your calendar, mark one-hour blocks of time for each task. If you've allocated two hours for one task, mark two one-hour blocks on the days leading up to your deadline.

4. Work your plan—before school.

   Why: To make sure you can get some chores done before you leave home.

   How: After breakfast at home, spend twenty minutes doing laundry, putting away clothes, or making your bed before you head to school. Check off completed tasks on your calendar list.

5. Work your plan—after school.

   Why: To make sure you complete your chores by day's end.

   How: Take a look at your calendar and note the hour blocks you reserved for your chores. Work on your chores for an hour. Keep tabs on your progress.

Remember, though you have many things to juggle, you need to meet your own needs as well as your family's. Staying organized with a calendar at home can help you and your family stay on track during the week.

Think About It   When we forget to do homework or fail to prepare for a test, there are consequences. We get bad grades. When we forget our equipment for practice or fail to run our drills or exercises, then we get benched and don't play. And with consequences often comes conflict. Why would this be any different at home?

It really sucks when we lose track of what we have to do for the day! Remember, it also sucks for your team. If you do your work at the last minute, your family has to put up with a stressed-out, sleep-deprived ADDYTeen. And that ADDYTeen may also compound the issue by screaming at family members that it is *their* fault the work is done late, because the family made the ADDYTeen empty the dishwasher. And this may have happened twenty times in the past year. At the end of the day, our actions affect not only us, but also the whole team—our whole family. If you can remember that your actions (or failure to act) have consequences for many, you are more likely to focus on meeting your responsibilities.

You can control the controllables, but you can't control the number of things people give you to do. Still, once you accept an obligation, you can control how you get it done.

Avoiding Procrastination

By now you have probably learned the word *procrastination*. What does it mean?

- Doing less-important tasks before more urgent ones

- Doing easy, fun things rather than difficult, less pleasant ones

- Putting off a task or chore to a later time

Yes, procrastinating is kind of like being lazy. Home is a *great* place to procrastinate. First, there are lots of other things to do. Second, there is often no clear deadline for getting tasks and chores done. At home the possibilities are endless. We can go to the kitchen and eat something. Then we can eat something else. We can go into the bathroom and groom ourselves endlessly. We can hang out on the bed, grab a device, and connect with the world. There are so many things we can do at home other than our work!

Heads up, ADDYTeens: you don't have enough time in your life to procrastinate. Not fair? Get used to it—you will never have enough time in your life to procrastinate. You must learn to use time wisely.

Think About It Sure, many put off work that they'd rather not do in favor of fun activities. Home can be tough for ADDYTeens, with lots of distractions and no clear schedule. ADDYTeens have brains that push us toward what's most interesting at the moment. If our brain is looking for fun or relaxation and we have chemistry homework to do "sometime today," generally fun and relaxation will win the battle of the brain cells. Then you face anxiety from waiting until the very last possible moment. The problems with procrastination are obvious: you wind up getting your work done late or done poorly, or not getting it done at all.

Why Do We Procrastinate?

First, answer this, honestly: Do you secretly enjoy procrastination? You get to do what you like, and then you compress all your work into just a little time. You get to do a lot of fun and a little work. Who wouldn't enjoy that?

Next, answer this: Does procrastination work for you? Well, there is some stress, of course, when you are doing your work at the last second. But if the time is compressed, you focus and buckle down and don't waste time, and when you finally get the work done it feels great, in part because the stress hormones can raise your blood sugar and have other effects that temporarily make you feel better. And wow, doesn't it feel great when it took you an hour to do the project and it took other people a whole week?

So you can be ambivalent about procrastination. You sort of want to get to your work. But part of you pulls away from that resolve because that part of you feels procrastination is actually good in some ways.

Let's Hear from ADDYTeens

Andrea, sixteen, had a *huge* procrastination problem. When asked if she procrastinates, she burst out laughing: "All the time!" and her parents did a big eye roll. She did say that she wished she would do this less. However, she admitted she actually loved the feeling of getting a lot of work done in a little time. "It takes everybody else two weeks to write a ten-page paper—I did it in two hours!" That made her feel great in some ways, although she also noted she felt panicky and upset with herself when she realized she had only two hours to do the work because it was due! And she agreed that her paper, although somewhat decent, did not represent her best work. After some discussion, she realized that what she actually liked about writing a paper in two hours was that she felt so focused when she did it. She realized how much better it would be if she wrote the paper in two hours when it was first assigned and then came back to it with the time she had left to make revisions and edits. Her grade in Language Arts went up a whole grade, and she felt a lot more in control. And no more eye rolls from her parents!

If you secretly enjoy procrastination, and if there are good parts about it, then what's the problem? D'oh! So many problems. First, do you want to be a success? Do you want to achieve your goals? Do you think great artists, businesspeople, athletes, and intellectuals you admire procrastinated their way to success? Face this part of you and get it out of your life. Remind yourself that you really, really do want to do a good job and you really, really don't want the stress of last-minute work.

How to Stop Procrastinating

Suit up, ADDYTeens! Recognize that procrastination will not work for you and will not help you reach your goals in life. To help you get out of this hole, here are three main ways to tackle procrastination in your home life:

1. Removing distractions

2. Managing electronics

3. Breaking down tasks into smaller steps and getting started with just the very first, then the next, then the next (managing your time)

If you can address these issues, you are guaranteed to reduce procrastination, if not cut it out completely.

Removing distractions is simple: we've already coached you to manage your environment, so you can remove distractions, cut through procrastination, and be productive.

-   Make your current environment more likely to help you concentrate than to help you goof off.

-   Change your environment: go to your school or public library, a dedicated learning place where it is quieter, and many distractions are eliminated.

-   Oh, and if you're easily distracted, avoid coffee shops or other busy areas!

How have I managed to do better at college than in high school? I live in the library, where it's quiet and I can focus.

Managing your electronics is a huge part of avoiding procrastination. Electronics and all the diversions they offer compete for your attention. Doing your chemistry homework versus Instagram? Instragram will win. That makes it harder for you to get your stuff done, not easier. So…

- Turn off your phone and leave it in the car trunk or your closet for a while.

- Use one of the many procrastination-prevention apps (consider AppDetox, StudyRails, or SelfControl) to set your own limits on how many times you can launch Instagram, or block out times of day when you can't activate the distracting programs. You may not want your parents to be the people managing your electronics. Do it yourself.

Take Action Managing your electronics is the single greatest way you can take action against procrastination! The number one cause of procrastination that Dr. Sarah hears about in her office these days is electronic distractions. ADDYTeens frequently tell her they are on their devices only because their ADHD prevents them from getting started; because they can't make themselves start work, they are on their devices. If only their ADHD could be fixed, they say, they would not be on their electronics. But it is not just that. The electronics are actively pulling them away from what they are supposed to do. This happens to everyone—not just those with ADHD.

The electronics industry has put a lot of thought and money into making sure that the programs you get hooked on are super compelling. Electronic devices and the social media they suck you into are part of the problem. They interrupt you even when you are planning on working (your friends call or text). Even when you are not playing a game, your phone may remind you that people are waiting for you to take your turn in a game. And you can't look at just one video on YouTube—the right-hand part of the screen always suggests new videos you might want to view. You are essentially being bossed around by your electronics (your phone yells "check Instagram!" and you cave in). *No bueno!*

Why let these entities boss you around? You have the power to manage your life and decide what you want to do and when!

Take action—it's simple:

1. Acknowledge that electronics actively pull you away from your work.

2. Decide to do something about it.

Winning your race begins with the first step. Remember the first three steps of the Foundational Play: Managing Your Time?

Step 1: Schedule Your Deadlines

Step 2: List Required Tasks

Step 3:   Plan Your Work

When you are feeling stuck or are having a hard time starting work:

- Make a list. Think, *What* can *I do?*

- Break down whatever you are going to do into tiny
  chunks. And we mean tiny. If we are talking thirty
  math problems, the first task would be walking to
  your desk. Can you just open the document? Can you
  just write your name on it?

- Just *start.*

If you find yourself telling yourself (or others), "I'll start in
ten minutes," then you are procrastinating!

Instead, practice saying in a determined voice, "I'm starting it
now, and I'll take a break in ten minutes" (or something similar).
When you just focus on the *starting* of the work, that one tiny
little step to start, it will make you less anxious. You are thinking
about only a little bit at a time.

- Don't think about how many hours you have in front
  of you. Think about the next ten minutes.

- Consider following the (10+2)x5 procrastination hack
  recently popularized by blogger Merlin Mann. You
  work in ten-minute bursts, each followed by a two-
  minute break, repeated five times in an hour.

You can do it! You have done harder things; you have endured
more pain; this will not kill you.

Once you establish new good habits, they will be as easy to follow as your old bad habits.

Remember, this is about becoming the person you want to be! Think who that person is and the goals you want to achieve. Write this down and post it in the place where you do your homework.

Talking with Parents

Parents can be helpful—sometimes. Not always. So it's super important to keep the lines of communication open to make sure your relationships stay healthy. Remember, we ADDYTeens often have emotions on steroids, and we can be a pain in the butt (be honest: it's true, right?).

When parents try to help, you may get mad. Sometimes— because, after all, they are *your* parents—you get more annoyed with them than you might with an unrelated well-meaning adult who is trying to help you. Other times you just don't need their help. Parents often think their role is to protect and help us, driving them to remind us about assignments, getting that sports equipment together, or collaborating with teachers.

However, as an ADDYTeen, it's your job to become more and more independent, so by the time you leave for college you are ready to manage yourself. So keep the following in mind:

- *Be polite and listen; do not interrupt.* You may decide you don't want their help or suggestion, but you must allow them to communicate with you if you want to be able to communicate with them. Your parents may be frustrated with you. Sometimes you want help, sometimes you don't, and either way you want to bite their heads off. Bad situation for all involved.

- *Be clear and calm.* You may feel like they are looking over your shoulder, micromanaging you, even spying on you, whereas they may feel like they are only trying to help. Help them know (calmly and pleasantly) what's helpful and what's not. When your parents get daily emails from computerized school programs (such as School Loop or PowerSchool) letting them know what is due in the next week, what your grades are, how many missing assignments you have, do not be surprised when they start to micromanage. Be clear about what you need help with and what you need to do yourself.

- *Reject guilt trips.* Some parents may make you feel bad about receiving their help. "When I was your age," they may say, "I was way more responsible than you are." They may make you feel that you should be able to do everything by yourself and that you are weak if you ask them for something. Be clear that this does not help—instead, it hurts—and if they want to help you, that is not the way to do it. Remind them you are not the same people, and they should accept you as you are and help you become *your* best self.

- *Show them your calendar.* Parents have no way to know how busy you are if you don't make it clear to them. If you feel you don't have the time to do chores at home as they insist, show them what you are doing with your time.

- *Earn their trust.* When you lie to or mislead your parents, about school or your social life, they will find out. If you want to be trusted, you need to be trustworthy. They may weigh in on who you should or should not hang out with or date. They may not trust you with certain people in your life; they may not trust you due to concerns about drugs, alcohol, or other issues. Talk this out calmly, see their point of view, and share yours. You may not agree with each other, but you won't both be angry.

- *Parents are imperfect.* You may be very frustrated with your parents. Or maybe you communicate well with one of them, and it's just the other one you find irritating. Maybe your parents are divorced, and one of them is stricter than the other. You are not perfect; neither are your parents. Deal with it.

- *Write it down!* Try writing your thoughts and feelings down as a letter or note. This is a great way to get your message across without feeling you have to battle your parents again. Slide it under their door or hand deliver it to them whenever you feel like you can discuss the topic again. When emotions flare up like giant fireworks, and everyone is upset, there isn't any point in continuing the conversation, because neither party will be able to actively listen.

What's an ADDYTeen to Do?

What do you want your relationship with your parents to be about? If you don't want it to be dominated by whether you did your homework or chores, think of other ways to connect with your parents that are not about school or housework. Take a walk, play catch, or play a game. Get manicures, see a ball game. Paint pottery at an art studio. Go to a music concert, museum, or play. (Hey, you might learn something useful.)

Your parents definitely say things they don't mean to say. Even when they say they are going to stay out of certain situations, there may be times they don't. Sometimes you can forgive them. Other times you need to be firm with them. Sometimes one parent respects the rules of the dynamic and the other doesn't.

Let's be real—it's hard to ask your parents for help when you frankly don't want to take the extra steps to do the work they suggest. I wished I was able to get my work done at home without questions or needing extra help understanding the instructions for a complicated assignment. Even when I needed help the most, I couldn't allow myself to stay calm and listen to their advice or guidance.

Who wants to have a constant tug-of-war with their parents? Communicating with parents at home can be especially frustrating after a long day. Over the years, I've had to practice talking to my parents in a way that gets my point across but also leaves space for them to speak their minds. This was vital, especially because I was notorious for getting upset and blowing up. Oops.

Practicing talking to my parents was incredibly helpful because I needed to understand the best way to express my thoughts and feelings without escalation.

One very important lesson I've learned is simple yet robust: communicate when you are calm.

Remember AID and these five points:

1. Try to calm down before talking about important issues.

2. Try to be clear and specific.

3. Keep the discussion to *one* particular instance.

4. Try to keep your words specific, such as "You did not listen when I told you that I would take the dogs out for a walk at 6 p.m. and not 5 p.m." instead of "You never listen to me! I told you I would get to it."

5. Write it down! Communicating with your parents face to face sometimes doesn't work.

Sharing your feelings and speaking up for what you need around the house can be challenging, especially if emotions run high. Nevertheless, talking calmly with your parents, whether it be about limiting distractions during your homework time or asking to get out of a chore, is a great way to get your message across and have them understand your point of view.

Consider this situation: You finish dinner and are about to start your homework when your dad turns on the TV at full blast. Next, your sister invites her friends over. Now your dog is barking at the squirrels outside. As much as you need to get your homework done, you are distracted by the activities in the house. You want to tell your family members to quiet down, but you don't know the best way to approach this conversation. It's time for this Set Play.

Set Play: Sharing and Advocating with Parents for a Quiet Study Place

1. Find a time when both you and your parents are free to talk.

   Why: To make sure you and your parents are attentive and present.

   How: Ask to talk to parents after dinner, before homework, or when you get home from school.

2. Explain your goal.

   Why: To ensure that they understand your intentions and the importance of your request.

   How: Directly voice what you'd like to accomplish and why removing distractions is important:

   - "I feel that I'm easily distracted a lot, and I need extra help staying focused."

   - "When I start to do my homework, all the noise I hear around the house is distracting."

   - "I need to get up less and be less distracted when I start my homework after dinner."

3. State your request.

   Why: To make sure your parents get it.

   How: Be specific: "Hey Mom/Dad, can you watch your TV show upstairs? The noise is distracting me from my work."

4. Justify your request.

   Why: So your parents understand why distractions have such an impact on you.

How:

- "If I could complete my chores *after* I'm done with my homework, I would be able to get a head start on my work."

- "If I could work in Dad's office after dinner instead of in the dining room, I would be able to close the door and limit my distractions."

5. Make an agreement.

Why: To make sure you and your parents are on the same page and they'll act to limit distractions.

How:

- "If I can complete my chores *after* my homework, I won't give an excuse for why I can't do them."

- "If I can work in Dad's office with a closed door, I will give you my phone until I'm done working."

You have to speak up for what you need from your parents in many different situations. Try the preceding Set Play to talk with your parents about:

- Getting a tutor

- Scheduling your chores

- Changing your curfew

- Improving communication around the house

Help! My Family Annoys Me!

We all get annoyed by our family. Even the best parents can be truly annoying. And siblings? "Annoying" seems to be part of their job description. As a teen, you want to be more independent. However, ADDYTeens often have issues they need to work on before they can achieve this. And that's annoying too!

Some family issues are about control. ADDYTeens want to do things their own way—but it may not be the best way objectively. When your family wants you to change your ways, it can lead to conflict, and everybody gets annoyed.

> **Dr. Sarah Says**   There are some biological factors that help explain why teens get annoyed with their parents. One major one is that many teens don't get enough sleep due to homework and early start times for school. Being short on sleep will make just about anyone irritable! Also, ADDYTeens tend, in general, to be quicker to anger than teens who don't have ADHD. This is part of the biology of ADHD—lack of impulse control—but it is not a license to get angry whenever you want. You need to know you may have this tendency and watch out for it, because you can get irritable not only at your parents (and they often take it) but also at your friends (who may stop being friends with you, because they have a choice!).

Let's Hear from ADDYTeens

OMG! Ellie, fifteen and a sophomore in high school, felt that her family was the worst. Although a small part of her knew they meant well, the overwhelming part of her wanted her parents to just "get away." She was smart, but never organized, and continually running late. She ran late on everything: going to school, going to softball practice, and most of all, doing her homework. Although in freshman year she made a few improvements, she still had her issues. Her family would try to give her hints—and sometimes orders—about how to get with the program. Her mom felt that if she would just do it *this* way, everything would be easier. But Ellie didn't want to do it *this* way, partly because her mom had already asked her to do it *this* way and Ellie was just mad that her mom had even brought it up. But her mom was concerned. Now that Ellie was in high school, grades counted toward college—for which her mom was working hard to come up with the money. Who should "win"—Ellie or her mom?

Ellie's mom got annoyed because her ADDYTeen was not taking advice and not doing what was needed, for no apparent reason. Ellie got annoyed for many reasons: her efforts were underappreciated, her mom demanded too much of her, and, after all, it's Ellie's homework and Ellie's grades, not her mom's. She felt like her mom just didn't understand or sympathize and was treating her like a little girl. Also, with her very full life between homework and friends and sports and procrastination, she often didn't get enough sleep, which made her even more irritable. Family therapy helped Ellie and her parents recognize when it was OK for parents to step in and help, and when it was better to stay back and let Ellie be Ellie. Ellie started to recognize when she was really being irritable for no reason—and how a lack of sleep contributed to that.

Let's be clear: You may not like how your family works. You may or may not be able to help make changes. Either way, you still need to manage your life and your ADHD. Start by being honest with yourself.

- Families get annoyed. It's usually not just your parents' fault or just your fault that you are annoyed. Often, it's both.

- Families have bad habits. Annoying patterns often develop over the years to the point where they become automatic.

- Your parents may have had bad training. Some parents never learned good parenting strategies. They may be just repeating how they were parented, and they don't know how to adapt.

- You are different. Sometimes there are personality mismatches. For example, it's hard when an overly worried mother has to parent a relaxed, "likes adventure" kid.

- It's their job. Your parents and siblings may be trying to protect you when you don't want to be protected. Listen to them, because you and your friends are more likely to think your ideas are good even if they are not.

> **Dr. Sarah Says** Remember that ADHD is often inherited. One of your parents (and/or siblings) could think in an ADHD way a lot of the time. Sometimes this is good for you— they may give you empathy and a lot of help. Other times their attitude might be *I survived without help; my kid just has to buck up like I did.* Still other times, they may be upset with you (even though you are acting like they do) because they are upset with themselves. It's hard for a parent to see a child make mistakes similar to ones they've made. So sometimes your ADHD parent will push you and push you because they feel they underachieved and they don't want you to. Either way, your parents are your parents; take the bad with the good and the good with the bad!

ADHD at home can be worse than ADHD at school.

At home it's easier to procrastinate. There are more distractions. Again, there is less structure: you get your responsibilities and homework done when you can. Often everyone has a different routine at home: you may be doing homework when your brother is at practice and your little sister is watching a movie. If you get angry at your brother or parents—well, that happens a lot, and one more time is not usually a big deal. School has a strict routine: this is classroom time for subject A, this is classroom time for subject B. At school you can look around and see others paying attention and working. And while you may get irritated at your teachers, you rarely lose your temper with them as you do with your parents. So you need to be extra-aware and proactive about the way ADHD can mess up your home life. Manage it!

You say you certainly *do* get irritated with your teachers? We're going to tackle that—and all the other aspects of winning with ADHD in school—in the next chapter.

chapter 5

ADHD at School

Most ADDYTeens first learn about their ADHD at school or because of the many challenges school brings up in their home lives. I learned about my ADHD as I transitioned to middle school. Other ADDYTeens discover their learning differences in high school.

We know—every ADDYTeen in middle and high school is doing a juggling act. Six or seven different subjects and teachers; clubs, plays, sports teams; homework, tests, projects, due dates; not to mention after-school activities and a social life! There are new relationships, new challenges at home. So many competing priorities, deadlines, and obligations. And maybe you don't get enough sleep either. In this chapter, we are going to help you keep all these balls in the air so you don't drop so many.

The idea behind this book, of course, is that you learn the skills you need to be successful in any situation, including school. But does that mean that you must learn them all in one day so you can be ready for the whole school year? Not at all. Realistically, it takes years to master these skills. You have some time!

Accommodations: Yes or No?

Heads up, ADDYTeens! Everyone has different strengths and weaknesses. There are some skills ADDYTeens need to learn and eventually master—skills that are not naturally our strengths. Our strengths tend to be creativity, thinking outside the box, finding new ways of doing things. These strengths are generally not prized (or graded) in school. Bummer, right?

Most schools reward students for good organization, being detail oriented, being careful and checking answers, being prepared and attentive, completing homework assignments right on time, and handing them all in as required.

Wow! These are things ADDYTeens are not naturally good at doing—so you need to learn skills. No fear; you can do it. Remember, the only way you get better at something is to focus on it, get help with it, practice it, and keep repeating it.

Your coach tells you this in basketball and soccer practice. Your director tells you this in band or theater. We are telling you this here—organization and time management are not easy to learn or to master, so you have to practice our Plays, repeat, practice, repeat.

This will take some time, so what can you do to improve your success at school?

ADDYTeens often need official *accommodations*. What exactly are these, and are they good or bad?

- Accommodations are a kind of compromise on the rules that are agreed upon for you, which allow you some time to improve.

- Accommodations are intended to decrease stress on you so you can develop skills that rely on focus. Some kids find focusing easy; ADDYTeens do not.

- Accommodations are at an administration level, to set up rules teachers *must* follow. Without accommodations, some teachers will give you help and others just won't. With accommodations, teachers *must* provide help.

For example, the general school rule might be "everyone has to get their homework done on time or they get penalized." You may have an accommodation that up to five times per year you are allowed to turn in homework one or two days later than your classmates. The idea is that, given this leeway, over time you will come up to the same level as the other students.

Here are some other common accommodations:

- Extra time (usually 25 to 50 percent extra) to take tests

- Taking tests in a less distracting or quieter environment away from others

- Being able to schedule your core classes in the morning when you are more likely to be focused

- Being able to get up and move around the classroom if you feel restless

- Less homework (if you take a long time to do homework)

- A special class with a teacher who helps you get organized

- Getting lecture notes from the teacher in advance so you can follow along in class already knowing what's being discussed

ADDYTeens: you can get help at school, and you should seek it out. It will help you perform at your personal best—and that is your goal, right?

Think About It We know some ADDYTeens refuse to consider any accommodations at all, even if they really would benefit from them. They don't want anything special done for them. They don't want to stick out.

Would you act like this at football practice? Heck no. You want to perform your best, so you ask for help. School is no different, people—no need to be ashamed of asking for help.

Why would you think school is so different from sports? When you are practicing a sport, you get coaching—help, guidance, instruction. Each player is given the same skills to learn, but the coach works directly with each player. It would be weird if you didn't ask for help from a coach. And even the very best athletes in the world have coaches—or, more likely, teams of coaches. It's not just sports, either; the same holds for music lessons, art lessons, any skill!

On the field or in the gym, getting help from your coach is ordinary, asking for help is ordinary; in fact, asking for help is required.

For ADDYTeens, school is no different. To perform at your best, you need some help. No biggie! There are helping hands along the way. Seek them out.

Accommodations is not a bad word—it's not something to be ashamed of. It's all in how you look at it. Try to look at accommodations as a way to make you become more competitive, to perform better, to learn new tricks and techniques.

How Do Accommodations Work?

Accommodations help remove the heavy rocks from your backpack—as we have been saying, you need ways to lighten the load. Instead of starting a school year at a disadvantage, accommodations give you a more even start by giving you time to develop the skills needed to make up for some of your weaknesses. Everyone has weaknesses, no biggie.

Here is what you need to know. There are two types of accommodations: 504 Plans and Individualized Education Programs (IEPs).

- 504 Plans refer to Section 504 of the Rehabilitation Act of 1973, a federal civil rights law to stop discrimination against people with disabilities, which range from disadvantages like ADHD or dyslexia to more serious handicaps like blindness or quadriplegia.

- IEPs are governed by the Individuals with Disabilities Education Act (IDEA), a federal special education law for children with disabilities. Both plans are free of cost to parents. Most kids with ADHD who need accommodations get a 504 Plan.

The biggest difference between a 504 and an IEP is that an IEP covers individualized special education for someone who requires it.

- Most kids with IEPs have learning disabilities like dyslexia, serious emotional issues, or physical impairments to vision, hearing, speech, or movement.

- A 504 Plan, in contrast, covers changes to the learning environment so that the general environment meets the learning needs of the student. That is where ADHD falls, because most kids with ADHD do not need individualized special education.

Your 504 Plan provides services and changes to the learning environment to meet your needs as adequately as other students'. A 504 Plan is provided at no cost to parents.

- If you get very distracted during tests, then you may, under your 504 Plan, be allowed to take tests in a quieter, more private room.

- If you need to be super careful reading instructions or checking your answers, your 504 Plan may also give you extra time to take the tests.

- If it takes you longer to produce, edit, or proofread your work to do your personal best, your 504 Plan may provide you with some flexibility to occasionally turn in some homework late or complete less homework.

- Your plan may give you an extra class period with a teacher there who helps you organize.

To get the process of accommodations started, talk with your school guidance counselor or principal. Your doctor may need to write a letter of support, but you get the accommodations from your school.

My Accommodations

I received a 504 Plan soon after I was diagnosed with ADHD. At first, I thought my accommodations would make me seem like a faker or dumb, but I soon realized how much they actually helped me in school. Taking tests in a more private room with limited distractions helped me with my test anxiety and trouble staying focused. Having extra time on tests helped me stay cool, calm, and collected rather than rushing against the clock.

However, I also had to learn how to advocate for myself and other resources I needed to succeed. Throughout high school I met every semester with all of my teachers, counselors, and my parents to talk about how the school year was going, my progress in each class, and how I felt about the support I was receiving. I used accommodations all through middle and high school and college. I truly believe that only stubborn people don't ask for help when they need it.

Even if you go to private school, the laws still apply to you, and your plan may be written through your public school system. Your private school may give you similar accommodations. If your needs are too great, however, the private school may not be able to give you enough accommodations; these would then be provided through the public school. One reason to get a 504 Plan is that it also helps you get accommodations for taking standardized tests such as the SAT or ACT (with extra time, a low-distraction environment, and so on).

Dr. Sarah Says You can get accommodations for high school, college, and even graduate school. However, after that the accommodations stop. Most people would not have accommodations for ADHD in their working life, and certainly your family doesn't give you any! So, get the accommodations, but make it a goal to use them less and less over time.

Take Action

* Go through the list of accommodations given earlier in this section.

* Write down what might be helpful for you.

* Make an appointment to talk with your school guidance counselor or the principal.

Asking Teachers for Help

Whether in middle school, high school, or college, as an ADDYTeen you must know how to communicate with your teachers and advocate for yourself and whatever resources you might need. You may have many questions and concerns about lectures, homework, tests, and due dates. Whether in or outside of class, the next Set Play is one to use when talking to your teacher.

Set Play: Applying an Accommodation to an Upcoming Exam

Imagine this situation: You have a 504 Plan—and an upcoming math test. You are allowed to take the test in a private room and have extra time to take it, but you haven't yet talked to your math teacher about applying these accommodations to your class. The test is coming up in two weeks, and you want to discuss with your teacher how these specific accommodations would apply to your test. Follow this process step by step!

1. Schedule an appointment with your teacher.

    Why: To have a private conversation.

    How: Approach the teacher and ask for an appointment.

2. Assemble persuasive arguments for accommodations.

    Why: To clarify your meeting goals.

    How: Write your goals on a piece of paper or in your notebook; for example, "I want to have more time to demonstrate what I've learned."

3. Confirm your need for extra time on tests and a private testing room.

   Why: To make sure your teacher knows what you'd like to accomplish.

   How: State what you'd like to accomplish.

4. Justify your need for accommodation.

   Why: To ensure the teacher understands why you need extra help.

   How: Bring documentation or an academic counselor's note that justifies accommodations.

5. Make an agreement with your teacher.

   Why: To make sure you and your teacher have a mutual understanding of your specific testing process.

   How: Record the agreement in writing; email it to your academic counselor.

It's essential to talk with your teacher. Some teachers, due to administrative mistakes, may not be aware that you have accommodations until you speak with them. And some teachers may be aware but are waiting for you to discuss the plan with them. You can tackle these situations with the same approach and steps listed in the Set Play. Try it out!

Managing Homework

Let's be honest: you get a lot of homework to do! Middle school, high school, and college all have multiple classes, teachers with multiple teaching styles—and so many deadlines! Having a plan to manage this homework is especially important for ADDYTeens because for most, it does not come naturally.

Managing homework involves being attentive to each class's assignments and deadlines, knowing how to time manage and organize, and executing and committing to a plan to get your work done. Hello! This all requires you to manage your time well.

The hard way is to try to remember everything in your head. Don't do it the hard way. Do it the easy way. Write. It. Down. As we discussed in chapter 3, for managing all your responsibilities and staying organized, planners and calendars are your best friends. For managing school work, they are essential!

Let's Hear from ADDYTeens

Fifteen-year-old Andrew was an ADDYTeen whose parents always told him to use a calendar. He thought it was just too much trouble; he said, "I can remember stuff." He was sort of right. He could remember *some* things. However, *some* things slipped through—*important* things, such as going to a best friend's quinceañera, meaning he forgot to get a present and forgot that it coincided with his soccer practice and studying for his final exam. He forgot scheduled lawn-mowing jobs. So finally, he took his parents' advice. He used Google Calendar. It was hard for him to get into the habit—sometimes he forgot to add things, and sometimes he forgot to check the calendar—he gradually improved. Now he can't imagine life without it. He observed: "Remembering things is the hard way to do it. Do it the easy way."

Organizing your homework assignments, papers, and class books is especially important because you know where everything is for the next day of school. We ADDYTeens are frequently messy and often lose handouts and homework assignments. Managing your papers involves managing your time, as discussed in chapter 3. Avoid clutter by using the next Set Play!

Set Play: Managing Papers, Assignments, and Books

1. Organize your homework tools and materials.

   Why: To make homework more efficient.

   How: Set out your calendar, colored pens, colored folders, and class syllabus on a table or desk.

2. Assign a colored folder to each class.

   Why: To keep assignments sorted and separated.

   How: Write on each colored folder the name of the class and the teacher.

3. Sort homework into three stages.

   Why: To help you differentiate old and new work.

   How: For each class, sort assignments into tabbed sections for those due this week, those completed for submission, and those returned to you.

4. Double-check and update folders after finishing homework and after school.

   Why: To make sure you have what you need for the next school day.

   How: Each day:

- Put each finished homework assignment into the "completed" section.

- Put each new assignment into the "due" section.

- Put each returned assignment into the "returned" section.

5. Dedicate work areas for class folders and textbooks.

Why: To make homework easy to grab before school and to find after school.

How:

- Store folders and books in the same places in your work area.

- After using any folder or book, return it to its place.

At some schools, teachers record assignments and instructions in a computerized program (School Loop, PowerSchool, Canvas, to name a few) that you can check at home. That can be enormously helpful—*if* your teachers are using it correctly. Some don't, though!

If you absolutely refuse to write things down, consider asking your teacher's permission to take a photo of the assignments she has written on the board. This is not as helpful as writing down assignments but it's better than nothing.

Managing Your Distractions at School

At school, the whole environment can be distracting. There are a bunch of people, all making noises, and one of the people is your teacher. And it's not just the people. From the posters on the walls to what you see and hear through the windows to the subject matter to your own thoughts...what was the teacher saying again?

How does your brain know which noise and which person to pay attention to? Well, managing your environment is a key part of that. Although you don't have a lot of control over your classroom, you do have *some*. Control the controllables, right?

- Control where you sit. Always sit in the front row. Yeah, we know that's not cool, but there is nothing between you and the teacher. You can see the board, and since the goal is to stay focused during class, you remove 90 percent of the distractions right there.

- Control who you're with. Do you think you can honestly concentrate better sitting near your goofball friends, or near where the quieter, more focused people sit? You can goof around or you can focus, but you can't do both.

- Control your actions. To help yourself pay attention, you might make it a goal to ask the teacher one question during the class. You can also experiment with how best to take notes. Some people get so focused on the notes that they don't really listen. Others find that writing things down helps them. There are Smartpens (such as Livescribe) that can record and transfer notes to laptops and other devices. If you have in-class work to do, try wearing noise-canceling headphones or earplugs. These are useful, but you may need permission to wear them. Similarly, you can stand up an empty binder on your desk so it blocks out some of your view of others.

- Control your attitude. Consider it your job to get focused and organized and do your best work. Take pride in your work. Run your best race—even with a heavy backpack, you can run strong. Show some grit. Be the person you want to become.

Oh, and the most important and unbreakable rule: don't take your phone out in class. Just don't.

Preparing for Tests, Papers, and Projects

Tests and projects require a decent amount of preparation that should start weeks before your deadline. Think of this like a soccer match: you wouldn't go onto the field before the game without training, preparing with your team, and being physically and mentally prepared as best you can. You need to practice before putting your skills to the test. What do soccer or basketball players do before their games?

1. Athletes must get to know their opponents and who they're playing against. As an ADDYTeen, you need to understand what lecture and course material will be included in the test.

2. Athletes must look to their coach for instruction, train individually to build specific skills and stamina, then

work as a team to practice plays. You need to communicate with your teacher about the test material, study the material on your own to get a good sense of what you know and what needs more practice, and then maybe meet with some friends or a study group to review and practice the material together.

3. Athletes must de-stress, get their head in the game, and concentrate on what they know and how to execute their skills to the best of their ability. Your process is the same. The practice part is over. Now you need to stay calm and execute the test in a way that reflects your preparation.

Bottom line: to execute well, *everyone* must prepare well.

The best studying is active studying. This involves action words like *doing* or *making*. It is making flash cards, for example, in Spanish class. It is making timelines, for example, in history class. It is doing practice problems, for math or science classes. It is *not* reading things over. Reading things over is the most ineffective way to study.

Cramming, whether for a test or a big game, doesn't work. Just as you can't build big biceps the night before a baseball game, you can't build big knowledge in your head the night before a test. Preparation for tests and projects involves working in steps over time to achieve the best results.

Dr. Sarah Says Feeling confident while taking a test is essential to focusing, and gaining that confidence starts with studying for it. Some ADDYTeens did not study in middle school but still did well on tests. That tends to change in high school, where tests require a deeper level of preparation. But many ADDYTeens find themselves at a disadvantage when taking tests because they're disorganized. They may forget they were having a test or, due to poor time management, not have as much time to study as they need. Not to mention that when they do study they may be working inefficiently. Active studying strategies like those described here help you reduce distractions and make every minute count.

Imagine this situation: You have a final test coming up in three weeks for your history class. You need to start preparing, but all the material you've covered and the length of the final test are making you put it off. There are many steps to preparing for a test, and you don't know where to start. The following material should help you start, keep pace on your work, and finish on time.

Taking Tests

Preparing for tests is half the battle; the other half is actually taking the test. During tests, ADDYTeens may find that distractions trigger "test anxiety"—feeling uptight, anxious, and forgetful during a test. It's true: I get more nervous taking tests than speaking to a two-hundred-person crowd.

Let's Hear from ADDYTeens

Kieran, fifteen, was a smart kid but did not do well on tests. He studied for them but was frequently disappointed in his scores. He knew the material but was distracted by what other people in the room were doing and how many times they got up. He worried that they were completing their tests faster than he was. Instead of focusing on the test problems, he focused on how much time was left and how *many* problems there were. The clock's ticking, his friend turning in his exam paper—every disturbance was highly distracting. Kieran was a very fidgety guy at the best of times, but when his fidgets combined with his stress and the stress of taking a test, he found it hard to stay in his seat.

Test Anxiety Is a Real Thing

Many ADDYTeens (myself included) deal with test anxiety for years. Learning how to cope is vital. I found accommodations very helpful: I was allowed to take my test in a private room with fewer things to distract me. I also was able to get extra time. That allowed me some time to relax and also to check my work for silly errors before turning it in.

If you can't get a separate room, what *can* you do? (In addition to actually studying for the test—feeling prepared will help you relax.) You can try to manage your emotions. Keeping your emotions under control while you take a test is one key to doing well. People worry about all sorts of things when taking tests. *What if I don't know the answer? What if I blank on a question? What happens if time is running out and I haven't finished my test yet? Why are other people finishing and I'm not done yet?* None of these worries helps you get the answers right.

Taking a minute to consciously relax at the beginning of a test can help. Try to do deep relaxing breathing or visualize something really fun. Visualizing something funny also helps, and if you can get yourself to smile, it will relax your whole body. It's likely that you have experience overcoming nervousness in many parts of your life—before a big baseball game, a music recital, or asking someone out. This is just one of those many parts.

When a test starts, scribble a few smiley faces on the test paper, to remind you to smile and relax periodically. Then, as the test progresses, every few minutes try to take a few seconds to relax. While you may be worried about taking too much time for this, know that this is a good investment of your time on a test—it will help you be less nervous and therefore think more clearly.

Always plan on taking the full amount of time allowed on a test—if you *plan* on being the last to finish, then you will worry less about competing with those who finish early. This way, even if you can't resist rushing through the test, you know you'll have to sit there and check your work. You are never going to do your best and finish a test early. Period.

If the test is not going well (hey, some tests are super hard!), remind yourself that you have prepared as best as you could. No one gets all the answers right. You can't control whether the test is fair (or the teacher grades it fairly). Control the controllables.

Set Play: Managing Your Time— Preparing for a Test

It's Friday afternoon in science class. Your teacher says in a week there will be a test on your textbook chapter 4. Follow these steps to prepare for your test.

1. **Schedule Your Deadlines.** Open your calendar to Monday and block off two or three hours each day that you will study for this science test. Color-code these entries, or any entries that have to do with your science test!

2. **List Required Tasks.** To prepare for the test, you need to review and practice.

   - Review means going through the chapter, revisiting your notes, and reviewing your homework, figuring out which material you get and which you don't get.

   - Practice means repeating the problems in your homework and sample problems listed in the book, focusing on those items you don't get.

   You can work on these with your teacher, tutor, parents, or friends, but the basic idea is to break a big job down into small tasks.

Grace's Play Tip

Even in college, I almost always need some type of help or clarification from my professors. In middle and high school, I always asked for help from my teachers. I learned that it's best to reserve some time with my teachers before an exam or a paper even before I knew what material I did not get. I wanted to make sure I had that time reserved just in case, and I almost always used it. For example, here is how I would use my planner/calendar to break down and plan for these tasks.

Task	Time Required
1. Organize materials—Get my book, notes, homework, and classwork for this chapter on my desk, ready to use.	15 minutes
2. Review chapter summary, class notes, and graded homework for chapter 4.	45 minutes
3. Review the sample problems in chapter 4. a. Put a yellow sticky note next to any problem that I don't get or that looks like one I got wrong on my homework. b. Put an orange sticky note next to those problems I get or got correct on my homework.	1 hour
4. Get help—Figure out which problems I still don't get, then ask my teacher or tutor for time to review. Work on those problems with my teacher again. (I may not get them all—my job is to do my very best work.)	1 hour
5. Work again on the tough problems I had asked for help on. a. Change the color of the sticky note to orange once I get it. b. Repeat—and visualize success during the test.	30 minutes
6. Review all the problems I get, and visualize success during the test.	30 minutes
Total time estimated	4 hours

Notice that I blocked off time in small chunks to prepare for this test, which is easier to manage than trying to cram for it one day before—and way less stressful. A little work up front to plan makes your life a lot better.

3. **Plan Your Work.** ADDYTeens, to manage your time it's best to work backward. You have a science test Friday at 1 p.m. That means you have to be ready for the test by Thursday at bedtime. Now, let's allocate the time you need to prepare and be ready for this test.

   a. Open your calendar to Tuesday of that week.

   b. Block off one hour and note: "Review all the problems I get and visualize success during the test." Highlight this.

   c. Block off one hour and note: "Review all the problems I don't get and sought help for and visualize success during the test." Highlight this as well.

   d. Do the same for Wednesday and Thursday.

Now that you have the hang of this, try applying these steps to your English or Spanish exam!

The Right Tool for the Job

Ever need to fix your skateboard or bike? Ever help your parents fix a fence, a sprinkler, a light switch? Doing these tasks requires tools. Yes, *tools*! Picking the right tool to perform a function or task is essential. You don't tighten screws with a hammer, and you don't use your bare hands either.

Planners and calendars are the right tools for time management and organization. Spend some time finding ones that work best for you. Relying on your memory to stay organized is like trying to tighten screws with your hands. It's the hard way to do it. It hurts, it's frustrating, and it's very ineffective.

Some ADDYTeens have a hard time writing things down in the planner during class—so what else can they do?

- Ask your teacher if you can take a picture of any assignments written on the board.

- Ask a friend who is good at using a planner to let you sync up your calendar with theirs—this is good practice.

- If your school uses an online calendar like School Loop, Powerschool, or Canvas, set an alarm to remind you to check this. Find a way to use it that works for you.

Dr. Sarah Says Students without ADHD may be able to automatically and quickly prioritize their different homework assignments. ADDYTeens, however, may see them all as equally important, so the workload feels overwhelming: we don't know where to start, so we don't start anything.

ADDYTeens are challenged to prioritize (figuring out what tasks must be done first, then doing them) and estimate (predicting the time needed to complete a task). These skills are essential to successfully using your planner—and completing your homework.

We tend to underestimate the time needed. Because we are so distractible, work can take a long time!

Here is a key strategy for honing your estimating skill: Look at your assignment (say, a set of math problems), estimate out how long it will take, and then time yourself. Set a timer when you start work. This also helps you focus better, because you've added interest (will you beat the buzzer?) and you have more of a stake in getting it done. If you make it, great. If it takes longer, you've helped yourself estimate more accurately the next time.

Set Play: Preparing for a Final Research Paper

1. Set a deadline.

   Why: To understand what you are working toward.

   How: In your calendar, mark the due date for your paper in bold or with a key color.

2. Break a big challenge into small parts.

   Why: To prioritize research tasks and avoid being distracted and overwhelmed by other tasks.

   How:

   - Determine which steps to do first.

   - Estimate how much time each task will take.

   - Mark each step and its allotted time on your calendar.

3. Commit to and work your research plan.

   Why: To time manage your whole project and stay accountable for your work.

   How:

   - Research and write every day for the exact allotted time.

   - If you fall behind, allocate more time for the next day.

4. Write the paper.

   Why: To tie together all the parts you've been working on.

   How:

   - Write an outline of the paper.

   - Input collected research/quotes into the outline.

   - Write topic sentences for each paragraph, then complete the paragraphs and integrate all.

5. Edit your paper.

   Why: To make sure your claims and arguments are clear and you've met all the paper requirements.

   How:

   - Read the paper out loud and mark sections for revision.

   - Do more research if needed.

   - For a quick outside review, make an appointment with your teacher or writing tutor.

Take Action   Here are some active study strategies:

* Make index cards throughout the semester, not just the night before the test. For example, each homework assignment you get those Spanish vocab words, make the index cards. For test prep, just go through them.

* As you are reading a chapter, write down questions you think might come up on a test. Save those questions! Test yourself later.

* For math, do practice problems as much as you can.

* For science, try to explain the concept to people (parents, siblings, friends) unfamiliar with the subject. If you can't explain something, you don't know it well enough yourself.

Make sure you have time to use these! When you put "test" on your calendar, block out study time in the days or weeks before. Consider "Study for test" an assignment to yourself.

Studying with Friends

Studying doesn't always have to be boring—studying with friends can be fun and productive!

When we think of studying, we think of reviewing class material to prepare for an upcoming test or project. Though experts say that preparing individually is the best way for you to learn and remember information, once you've learned and prepared yourself, reviewing the course material with some friends can help you integrate the information you've learned through different approaches and conversations.

Studying with friends in the same class helps me shift my thinking from detailed and narrow to the bigger picture. Tying the small specific topics I learned in my study guide to how they apply to more abstract concepts is super helpful. Others get the big picture easily on their own but find the study groups helpful for pointing out small details they are not yet comfortable with.

Give some thought to picking which friends to study with. How productive would it be to study with your best friend if you'd wind up just chatting about the latest and greatest? Not so good. Instead, choose classmates and friends to study with based on their understanding of the classwork.

Talking with your friends (or even your parents) about test material can help you prepare your answers to exam questions. Practicing your answers out loud will help you identify material you've mastered and other material you need to practice more. This is a perfect opportunity to identify your subject gaps and bring them to your teacher's attention. Your teacher can point you and your study friends in the right direction, which will make studying go a lot better. This also shows your teacher your engagement in the class.

Think About It   When you study with friends, they must turn off their electronics too; that is just how it works. It's a good study practice to remove distractions even if you don't have ADHD. But for ADDYTeens, it's 100 percent required 100 percent of the time.

Set Play: Studying for Tests with Study Partners

Imagine this: You have a history test coming up in two weeks. Studying vocabulary, geography, and famous travelers can be boring, so you want to practice with some friends in your class. Follow these steps to form a study group to master the material!

1. Set a goal of studying for the next week and a half.

    Why: To underscore what you are working toward.

    How: In your calendar, mark the test date and time in color or bold.

2. Study the test material individually before working with friends.

    Why: To be prepared to ask specific questions rather than reviewing the basic information you just learned.

    How:

    - Use flashcards, diagrams, vocabulary words, and a study guide; make your own or print your teacher's guide.

    - Spend at least six hours studying alone.

    - Identify what you know, what you're unsure of, and what you need to study or practice more.

3. Pick study buddies you work well with and plan a study session.

    Why: To have a chance to review the material aloud and to organize your study guide.

    How: Call your study buddies after school, see them in class, or text them, and suggest a time and date to meet at least four days before the test.

4. Fully prepared, meet with your study group.

    Why: To make the most of your time together.

    How:

    - Bring all your fantastic individual work to your group meeting.

    - Discuss what each of you knows, what you are unsure of, and what you need to study and discuss more in depth.

You must focus on what you can control, regardless of whether you use accommodations. You can control how messy your backpack is. You can control whether you are trying to do homework while Snapchatting. You can (usually) control where you sit in class. You can control your preparation for tests and how you take them. If you do your very best at these things and manage them as well as you can, then whatever grade you get in the class is a victory. You will have learned how to manage school. Class grades come and go; the class always ends. But if you learn the process of getting your work done, managing your emotions when you are nervous, and paying attention to people who can help you succeed in class, then you have learned important skills that you can apply to any situation you encounter.

chapter 6

ADHD and Friends

ADDYTeens, have you ever noticed that ADHD can sometimes affect you socially? This can be a bummer during a time in your life when you want to present your best self to others. Communicating with others can be problematic in two ways: impulsively saying things you don't mean and not being a great listener. Talking and listening—that pretty much covers communication! Constant fidgeting and moving irritates some people. Also, if you find it hard to wait in line or wait your turn, you may find it hard to participate in group activities that involve waiting—in lines at amusement parks, for your turn at bat, or in the lunch line. Also, unfortunately, with all the ADHD challenges we're dealing with, anxiety and depression can creep in and affect friendships too.

I confess…I was a loud, hyperactive, impulsive child. For many years, making friends was a challenge, and keeping them was even harder. I would say things that were more hurtful than nice; I'd intrude on others' personal space. This got me into trouble.

So here are a few lessons from my experience.

Oops, I Didn't Mean to Say That (Communication)

We've talked about impulse control in prior chapters. What does this have to do with talking to others? Well, a lack of impulse control means we do things without thinking—and in the case of talking with friends, we say things without thinking. We've all said something we shouldn't have, hurt someone's feelings unintentionally, or blurted comments when we should have held our tongue. For ADDYTeens, this can happen a lot. We interrupt our friends, speak loudly to get our point across, even use bad language when we're stressed out.

Did you ever make a comment quickly, maybe to be funny, and later realize *Dang, that was mean!* That happens to everybody, but when you aren't thinking about what you are saying, it happens more. Impulsivity leads to a lot of "oops" moments, because when there is no filter between your brain and your mouth, embarrassing remarks can come tumbling out.

It may be hard to recognize at the time, but outbursts like this have killed many a friendship. We may, for example, think we have something extraordinary to say that is super important, but when we pull on our friend's arm to get their attention, we may just come off as annoying and distracting. It is important that when we are with our friends we behave the way we would want someone to act around us: cool, calm, and fun—not irritating, loud, and bothersome.

Thinking before you act is a big skill every ADDYTeen can work on. Truth is, I still work on it myself! It is way too common that we find ourselves misspeaking or acting inappropriately just because we don't take the time to "read the room." Heard of this phrase? Reading the room means that we consider where we are, who we are with, and what we are doing. This can help contextualize appropriate behavior.

And the other half of communication—listening—is often not one of our strengths, either. Sure, you can listen, but you tend to do so only when you are *really* interested in what your friend is saying. And that may not be as often as your friends would like.

Of course, people listen differently depending on the situation. You listen differently to teachers who are giving information (and you probably don't listen to teachers who are not). You may or may not care to hear what your parents are saying. However, most ADDYTeens know, on some level, that to be a friend they must be a good listener. The "fake listen"—meaning kind of listening, but kind of tuning in and out—doesn't work. "You never listen" is not a phrase that brings people together—it's often the prelude to a breakup talk.

The best listening happens when we keep looking at the person we are talking with and we really listen to what they are saying (not just thinking how we'll respond).

How can you become a better listener? First, look at the person you want to listen to. Your eyes tell your brain what to think about. If your eyes are on that person, your brain is much more likely to be on that person, and you are more likely to listen to them. If you are looking at your phone, your brain will go to the phone, or maybe jump back and forth between the phone and the person talking. Not the kind of listening we're recommending! So, put your phone away when talking with other people.

OK, think you've got it? Test your listening skills with the next Set Play.

Set Play: Impulse Control: Think Before You Talk

1. Choose the right *place* to share your ideas, thoughts, and feelings.

   Why: To understand the importance of setting for communication.

   How: Take note of where you are and who is around you. Are you playing outside? Working in a classroom? At soccer or basketball practice? Is it best to share these ideas in private or public?

2. Choose the right *time* to speak.

   Why: To make sure you have a receptive audience.

   How: Decide whether it is best to speak:

   - During class or at break
   - In a note or face to face

   Reflect in the moment and consider:

   - Are people already talking or is there an opportunity for me to speak?
   - Should I share this with the class or with someone privately?

3. Think about what you want to say and how to say it.

   Why: To become a more effective speaker and to make sure your points are clearly heard.

How: Even if you have something impactful to say, consider not only *what* you say, but also how. Stop to consider:

- Am I asking for help or clarifying a question?

- Does my comment contribute to the ongoing conversation?

- Are my thoughts or comments on or off topic?

- Will I distract others?

- Is this comment helpful or hurtful or distracting?

4. Fine-tune your communication.

   Why: To perfect your communication skills.

   How: Share your comments and ideas politely and directly.

   - In class, raise your hand and speak only when called on.

   - In a group of your friends, wait until someone has finished speaking.

   - When voicing a complaint, speak calmly and give specific examples.

Acting Appropriately (Behavior)

All teens must learn how to act appropriately, especially if they want to be respected by others. This includes parents, coaches, and teachers, but also your friends. Because having ADHD often involves impulsive behavior, hyperactive behavior, and procrastination, this is often difficult.

Impulsivity. In the previous section we discussed impulsively talking too much. Sometimes our actions can also be too impulsive.

- ADDYTeens sometimes push safe boundaries, skiing out-of-control fast, driving out-of-control fast, testing gravity by jumping off of things that we shouldn't jump off of.

- Other risky behaviors can include deciding to have sex without birth control or STD protection, and/or drug and alcohol use. Some of your friends may encourage these behaviors, but such friends don't have your best interests at heart. People who *do* care about you will be alarmed by these irresponsible and dangerous behaviors.

- On a more positive note, sometimes impulsivity can lead to fantastic and creative ideas. But stay safe, people!

Pushiness. ADDYTeens often can be too rowdy or pushy with our friends. This can get us into trouble.

- ADDYTeens may carelessly touch other people's stuff—or people themselves—without first asking permission.

- ADDYTeens sometimes can even get physically aggressive. You might get angry and then hit someone in a situation where someone without ADHD might have just yelled. That can get you into big, big trouble, and feeling really sorry later won't help.

Procrastination and forgetfulness. Remember our old friend, procrastination? Yeah, he is still here, with his buddy, forgetfulness. What happens when you make plans but forget to finish your homework or clean your room?

- We often have to cancel plans because we forget to take care of our tasks at school or at home. You don't like your time wasted, and neither do your friends!

- It's a big letdown for you and them when you have to cancel plans. And it's not always because we procrastinated. Sometimes we simply forget we made plans with our friends, or we double-book to hang out with two different friends. That is embarrassing!

Take Action: Read the Room   See yourself in these scenarios and decide how you should ideally behave:

1. Your friend Jim is in the library studying for an exam tomorrow, and you have a question about your plans with Jim this weekend.

   a. Interrupt Jim's focus and concentration to ask your question.

   b. Send Jim a text message.

   c. Make a note in your calendar to ask him later.

> **2.** As your study group prepares for an exam, your good friend Alexa seems upset and says something critical about an idea you shared.
>
> a. Ask her why she is acting rude.
>
> b. Ask her if something is upsetting her.
>
> c. Move on to the next topic; you and Alexa can talk after the group is finished.
>
> *With both of these questions, C is the ideal choice. In Question #1, if you choose A or B, Jim will be rightfully annoyed with you as you are not supporting his concentration. In Question #2, you are inviting interpersonal conflicts and distraction from the task at hand if you choose A or B.*

Keeping Yourself Together (Emotions)

Managing our emotions is a big part of making and keeping friends. Emotions can flare up even when our friends didn't do anything to cause it. So, it's important to recognize and identify our bombs and fuses—the sensitive topics that set us off. What rubs us the wrong way? Whatever it may be, what bugs us is not necessarily our friends' fault.

There are many situations that put me on edge. I could have a rough day, feel funky after my medicine wears off, or feel stressed about my homework. Though these things may give me a pretty short fuse, that doesn't mean it's OK to take things out on my friends. I wanted to avoid starting unnecessary fights with my friends, so I needed to learn how to identify my triggers—aka the things that set me off. Once I learned how, I could see how sometimes it was my medication or homework that was really making me mad, not whatever my friend just said. By learning to distinguish between your feelings in general and your feelings from your friends, you will enjoy better friendships and avoid the drama of fights.

Remember: control the controllables! Even if your friend does say something that makes you mad, you can't control your friend! But you can control your attitude and responses.

Now, let's say you do get into a fight with your friends. You might have blurted something out when you shouldn't have, acted a bit too rowdy for the moment, or snapped at your friends because you had a rough day. The most important part of a fight is working to resolve it.

Talking about your hurt feelings with your friends is a great skill, with the potential to make or break your friendships. It's crucial to express yourself with your friends, but in a positive and proactive way.

When sharing my feelings with a friend, I'm careful to use *I-statements*. Rather than focus on what the friend did wrong, I approach the conversation with how I felt and what bothered me, and why. When you use I-statements, it's important to then ask your friend how she or he felt in the situation in order to hear both sides of the story.

Recognize that your friend may have a point, even if the situation is annoying to you. Hear your friends out just like they have heard you.

When we manage our emotions and share how we feel with our friends, it makes it easy to move forward and not hold a grudge. Just as we learn to defuse the bomb of our intense emotions, we need to make sure that we're not holding onto any ill feelings toward our friends.

Set Play: Working Out a Problem or Resolving a Fight with a Friend

1. Identify your goal.

   Why: To help you stay focused and on topic.

   How: Explain what you would like to talk about, using I-statements; for example:

   - "I felt embarrassed when you asked Jill to dinner but not me."

   - "I felt hurt when you forgot our plans to hang out."

   - "I got upset when I heard you talk behind my back."

2. Select the person you want to talk to.

   Why: To help you gather your thoughts specific to the situation.

   How: Think about who hurt your feelings and why talking to that person would be helpful.

3. Request a time to talk.

   Why: To make sure you both have time needed to talk.

   How: Choose how you would like to contact this person:

   - Call, text, or in person.

- Ask if your friend would be free to meet and talk.

- Suggest a time and a place to meet.

4. Share your thoughts and feelings.

Why: To make sure your friend can understand where you are coming from.

How:

- Use I-statements.

- Speak slowly.

- Respect the other person's opinions.

- Return to your I-statements if needed.

5. Discuss how to move forward.

Why: To resolve the fight or disagreement.

How:

- Suggest two things *you* can do differently.

- Suggest two things *the other person* can do differently.

Social Anxiety and Depression

Let's face it: we ADDYTeens face a lot of hurdles many other people don't. Social situations can be just as challenging as school life and home life.

Having impulsivity can sometimes make us feel like outsiders. It's hard to be social when you are not sure how you will react to others, may not have the best commentary, or know that you are not the best listener.

Think about the kids in school who do the best socially. They move with an ease in their own skin. But for us, becoming confident socially can be very difficult.

Although ADDYTeens can be happy and bubbly, with zillions of friends thanks to the positive aspects of ADHD, many ADDYTeens have social anxiety—meaning they feel more uncomfortable in social situations than is considered normal. We may want to be social but fear it for a variety of reasons.

We may fear being judged or embarrassed, and we may become less social and therefore feel more isolated and unhappy. Or we may feel that social situations are so energy draining that we'd rather not try to be social. Netflix, video games, Facebook, and other solitary outlets are always there for us and often easier to manage than real-life people.

All of this can potentially lead to depression. And you know what? It's hard to make friends when you are depressed. You don't have the motivation to make the effort or spend the time. What's worse, depression makes it hard to put your best foot forward and be the most interesting version of yourself; other kids might not be able to see how much fun you actually are. If you play sports, this feeling might also lead you to quit the team, which can make depression worse. Not only will you get less exercise, but you also may lose contact with your friends on the team—some of them might even be mad at you for leaving them in the lurch before the big game!

Let's Hear from ADDYTeens

Alexander, fifteen, complained of feeling tired all the time, despite getting a reasonable amount of sleep. He blamed it on his divorced parents' shared custody arrangement. Every two months he stayed with his mom for a few days, and she wanted to do lots of activities with him, so he got behind and had to catch up on work afterward. However, he was still overly fatigued even when he wasn't even close to a visit. After some discussions and a few weeks in therapy, it became clear that he was feeling overwhelmed by his work and also felt that his friends were judging him. Therapy helped Alexander get a better handle on the real reason for his feelings of exhaustion, and he felt a lot more energetic and able to get work done.

Take Action What can you do to keep from getting socially anxious and/or depressed? Lots of things:

* Join a group where meetups are required. That could be a school play, robotics club, Girl Up, or another school club. If this group has a meaningful mission for you (a great play, a great robot, or doing good in the world), you will push yourself to go even when you don't feel like it. And it's nice to know that people there definitely share your interests and goals.

* Be sure to exercise. Exercise reduces anxiety and improves mood. Doing exercise with other people is great. Join the cross-country club and go for a run. Tap dancing or rock climbing, anyone?

* Try to protect your sleep. Lack of sleep compounds anxiety and depression. If you can't sleep well, let your parents and doctor know.

* Remember that electronic buddies are no substitute for real-life buddies. It's important to interact with people in the real world.

* If you feel anxious and depressed, getting out into nature can really help. Go for a walk. Appreciate a flower. Hike up a mountain or bike down a mountain. Throw a snowball, make a snowman, sing in the rain. Just get outside!

On a positive note, although we've just discussed how ADDYTeens can get pushed around or isolated, many can be super popular, "the life of the party." The energy and ideas that they bring to a situation are often very appealing. Their lack of inhibition makes them open to lots of ways to have fun. ADDYTeens may be daring enough to be star athletes, the main character in the school play, or the next student body president.

Look: our feelings are real to us, and strong emotions like anxiety and depression can be very challenging. We have been telling you clearly: it's OK to ask for help now and then. Everyone needs help from time to time. If you are unhappy or feel anxious or depressed, don't feel shame. Take action.

chapter 7

Medication

ADDYTeens, this whole book has been about your attitude, goals, and behavior. We've talked about managing ADHD with systems in place for home, school, and friends. And those systems are super important. But we also want to talk about medication for focus, because you know it is there, and some of you have tried it or are thinking about trying it. In this chapter, we'll give you a simple rundown of medications for ADHD and the issues about taking them.

ADHD Meds: Part of the Solution?

Medications for ADHD can be a part of living with your ADHD—but only a part. Why? Because ADHD meds help you do one thing: focus better. Think of medication as like a soccer player's cleats. Cleats do enable you to play at your best, because they give you traction. But cleats don't dribble or pass or shoot on goal. You have to do that. You can't play as well without them, but they do not know strategy, make decisions about whom to pass to, or summon up the drive to do your best. You have to actually do the work when you are focused.

Let's break it down:

- Medication helps you focus the way glasses help you see clearly.

    - Glasses don't do your homework for you, but seeing clearly makes homework easier.

    - ADHD meds don't do the homework for you, but they help you focus well enough to both start and finish your work.

- Medication helps you prioritize, which makes your use of time more efficient.

    - With ADHD, your brain has a hard time prioritizing one thought over others.

    - The medications make it easier for your brain to prioritize one task.

    - As one task stands out to your brain, other distractions become less prominent.

    - You are then able to do the tasks that need doing without as much distraction.

Neither the glasses nor the medication will do your homework, write your papers, or take your exams. You still need to manage your time, manage your environment, speak up for what you need, and improve how you interact with others.

Think About It   Hey, ADDYTeens: You play sports, do homework, write papers, and take exams. If you had bad eyesight, would you try to do all these things without glasses? Would you think that using glasses is cheating?

How Do ADHD Medications Work?

ADDYTeens and parents, we need to tell you a secret. Experts like Dr. Sarah and many others can tell you that ADHD medications can work, but they can't tell you why. The short and honest reason: we don't *really* know how the medications work because we don't *really* know how the brain works. Yes, we said that— even brain scientists don't really know how the brain works.

Here is what we do know:

- ADHD is not a condition that a doctor can see on an X-ray or MRI.

- ADHD is part of how your brain works, but doctors don't know exactly how ADHD changes the way that the brain's network of chemical messengers (*neurotransmitters*) operates.

- We know that the brain neurotransmitters *dopamine* and *norepinephrine* are involved in ADHD, because they are involved in most every brain function. Doctors don't exactly know what is different in how an ADDYTeen's brain functions, compared to a "regular" brain.

Note: if you read about ADHD on the internet, you may conclude that ADHD is caused by a dopamine deficiency. That is not true. Dopamine is a very complicated neurotransmitter, used all over the brain for many different functions, including attention, movement, and even breastfeeding! Dopamine is affected in some ways by the medications, but there are probably other neurotransmitter systems involved as well. It's better to understand how the ADHD medications differ from each other and to know that they work in some way, rather than get hung up on trying to figure out exactly how they work.

Here is what you need to know:

- There are two types of ADHD medications: stimulants and nonstimulants. Both types work well for all types of ADHD (inattentive, hyperactive, or combined).

- Stimulants (Ritalin, Adderall, Vyvanse, and Focalin) are the most common ADHD medications. The basic molecules in them have been in use for many decades. Even though they are called stimulants, they make ADDYTeens feel calmer and more focused. Your brain, rather than rapidly moving from one task to another, can stick with one task longer. Yep: like glasses, they make it easier to focus—possibly by increasing dopamine in certain areas of the brain.

- Nonstimulants (like Intuniv, Kapvay, and Strattera) have a similar effect, generally speaking, but through a different mechanism than stimulants use. Interestingly, some of these medications have been repurposed from their original uses and may influence dopamine also. For example, the basic active ingredients of Intuniv and Kapvay were first used to treat high blood pressure.

Which Medication Is Best for You?

Here is how Dr. Sarah explains ADHD medications to her patients.

Stimulants	Nonstimulants
Can be taken every day, or you can skip them on some days.	Should be taken every day.
Work right away.	Take a few weeks to work.
Last from a few hours to ten to twelve hours during the day. Some stimulants are fast in, fast out; others are slowly released over many hours.	Are in your system 24/7 (which may be good or bad, depending on your viewpoint).
Can have side effects—most commonly worse sleep, appetite, and mood, and increased blood pressure and pulse, both of which need to be monitored. Your doctor will also want to track height and weight to make sure these are not affected. They can also cause or exacerbate tics.	Can have side effects. These are more variable. Some tend to make you more sleepy, and there is less of an appetite suppression effect than with stimulants (although Strattera can cause nausea).
Are the most commonly prescribed, as they probably work the best for most people (but may not be the best for any one individual).	Some people can't take stimulants, for a variety of reasons, making nonstimulants their only choice. For those who can take stimulants, nonstimulants may be taken in combination with them or supplementally.

Let's Hear from ADDYTeens

Jaden, age fifteen, and his family were trying to choose a medication. It was mid-March, and one reason to try stimulants was that the semester's end was only a few weeks away, so the nonstimulants might not work in time for his finals. He was a skinny guy and concerned about losing weight on the stimulants, as he was actually trying to gain weight. Also, he was concerned that the stimulants might not work for him long enough during the day, as he tended to do his homework later in the evening because of baseball practice. After some discussion, the plan was to try a long-acting stimulant in the hope it would last late enough for him, and see how he did with his weight. Although he definitely felt some appetite suppression at lunch, he made sure to eat a big breakfast and dinner, and his weight remained at least stable.

The medication started to wear off for him about 8 p.m., so he tried his best to get some homework done before practice, so he just had a little work left to do most nights when the medication had worn off.

Dr. Sarah Says What about caffeine—coffee, black tea, caffeinated sodas? Caffeine is probably the world's most commonly used stimulant. However, it is not as specific or strong for focusing as the FDA-approved medications discussed here.

Medication—Yes or No?

So, let's focus on three points:

- What is the best type of medication for *you*? Your doctor will help you make choices about ADHD medication, and you may need to try out a few options. Be patient, especially with nonstimulants, which don't take effect for several weeks.

- Are the benefits worth the negatives of any side effects—for you?

- ADHD medications are not necessary from a medical viewpoint—that is, the ADHD is not a threat to your physical health (unless you are driving distractedly due to your ADHD). So you need to know that taking medication for ADHD is *optional*. You take medication *only* if you want to see whether it is helpful, and you keep taking it only if the benefits outweigh the side effects.

Like cleats, other sports gear, or prescription glasses, medications are best viewed as a tool in your toolbox. Other tools are your strategies for reducing distraction and increasing accomplishment, which may be your own personal tools (such as turning your phone off while you do homework so it doesn't distract you) or more institutional accommodations, such as taking tests in a less distracting environment.

Sometimes ADDYTeens or parents make a categorical statement: "I don't want medications." When you say this to your doctor, it's important to explain *why*. Are you philosophically opposed to all medications for ADHD? Or do you have a concern about them, such as knowing that the medication your friend was on made him too quiet or suppressed his appetite?

It's normal to have a lot of questions about ADHD medications. Many ADDYTeens may know somebody on medication. Whether to take medication is one of the toughest decisions that many ADDYTeens and their parents must make.

Many parents fear that taking medication will turn their child into an addict or make them reliant on the drug. If you can explain *why* you don't want medications, you can have an educated discussion with your doctor. After that, your answer may still be no, but with a better understanding.

When medications work well, they can be a powerful aid in winning with ADHD. And although they can give you side effects, they are safe medications for nearly everybody. So don't close the door until you understand what medications do or don't do, and how you may feel when taking them. Then feel free to reject them. Many do.

This book is all about changing how you live with and manage your ADHD. All the concepts, coaching, and choices we present are based on changing your behavior in order to succeed. Psychologists call this cognitive behavioral therapy (CBT). Essentially, it is a way to boost happiness and productivity by helping a person modify how they feel and think about their challenges and how they behave in response. CBT focuses on solutions, like the Foundational and Set Plays we offer here.

The U.S. National Institute of Mental Health (NIMH) sponsored a very large study, the Multimodal Treatment of ADHD study (also called the MTA), that compared kids who took medication only, got behavior modification therapy only, or did both. In the beginning phase of the study, medication really did seem to help. The symptoms of ADHD were improved quickly and effectively. However, over time the medication's effects became less notable, and more subjects stopped the medication.

Conclusion: Medication is not the solution to ADHD. Medication does help many ADDYTeens focus. But managing your ADHD takes strategies like our Plays. If you practice these, you will gain important skills and strategies. Then, with those strategies, you have some power over the ADHD and can get off of medication if you choose. These strategies are also helpful toward the end of the day, as the stimulant medications wear off. So whether you take ADHD medication, never take it, or take it for a time and then stop, you need to develop some strong behavioral strategies to rely on, like our Plays and coaching.

What Does Medication Feel Like?

For some ADDYTeens, the first time they take medication that works is a revelation. Some say, "For the first time, I know what being focused feels like," or even "I seriously don't mind doing my homework now." After all the frustrations of starting to work, then getting distracted, then starting to work again, then getting distracted again, it feels good to just sit down and get work done efficiently. Then anxiety about doing the work is eased, because it is not such a terrible experience. And you may find you're less inclined to procrastinate—it's easier to start doing work if you think it will be OK.

Many ADDYTeens describe ADHD as "too many things going on in my head." Taking medication reduces the number of different thoughts. Thoughts feel clearer and sharper—like your vision when you wear prescription glasses.

You may or may not "feel" the medication working. The idea is not to feel like a "work zombie." But you should definitely notice a difference in your ability to listen and to do work without making silly mistakes, and an improved ability to start—and finish—your work. Actually, one measure of the medications' effectiveness used in drug development trials is whether the number of math problems a subject does correctly in a certain time period goes up when subjects take the medication.

You shouldn't expect to feel like a super-focused super-hero. You should feel a difference in your productivity. Many ADDYTeens express this as "I finally know what normal feels like."

Be aware: some people express concerns that the medications are part of an effort to "mind control" children and keep them from being kids, or that teachers are recommending them so the teachers would have an easier job, or that parents are using them to make their children better behaved. If you have a real case of ADHD, like me, you know this is *not* true. Medication works for ADDYTeens so they can begin to achieve their goals and accomplish what they need to. As medications enable them to finally focus in a "normal" way, they find their self-esteem increasing. And *because ADDYTeens believe that they can succeed, they try hard—and then they do succeed.* Then their self-esteem goes up even more!

What to Do When Medication Makes You "Feel Weird"

Doctors, parents, and teachers would all agree: medication should not make you feel weird. With these medications being optional, you want to make sure the benefits are not outweighed by side effects.

One major concern that ADDYTeens have is "Will I still feel like myself?" The answer is honestly "Yes, but…"

- *Yes*, we want you to feel like who you are, and not to change the essence of your personality.

- *But* something has to change if you are going to improve your ability to get your work done. That something may be that you are less silly or talkative with others.

Friends may notice that, instead of returning texts at all hours of the day and night, you are turning your phone off to get homework done. Or instead of talking and joking with them during a class, you are actually listening to the teacher. You can't do both of those things at once! So there may be some aspects of the medication that you don't like, or your friends don't like, but the trade-off is that you are spending less time distracted.

There are ways these medications can make you feel weird. Some of the most common side effects are worse sleep, worse mood, and worse appetite.

- Everyone who takes these medications *could* have the side effects—but they may or may not actually have

151

them. And if you change to a new medication, you have a whole new set of potential side effects.

- Even if you stay within the same category (all in the stimulant category, for example), one medication's side effects could be different from another's *for you*. That's one reason there are so many of these medications out there. There is no single one that works (or has fewer side effects) for everybody.

Here is what you need to know:

- For some, stimulants can make it harder to get to sleep; others may wake up more during the night. In contrast, Intuniv, a nonstimulant, can make you more sleepy.

- Stimulant medications tend to lower your appetite (generally seen as a problem by more boys than girls). Weight loss can happen, but more commonly, people don't eat much during the day and then make up for it by eating a whole lot in the evenings. A lower appetite is a problem if it leads to too much weight loss, or you're being cranky because you have not eaten.

- Medications can also make your mood worse in just about any way you can think of—more angry, more sad, more worried. If people say you are irritable, you are! Don't just yell at them that you are not irritable; remember that you might be, and it's not you, it's the medication. Medication can improve your mood also, if you are accomplishing more.

ADDYTeens! If you don't like your medication, guess what? You. Can. Stop. Taking it.

Just communicate with your doctor so they can tell you how to get off your medication safely. It is safe to simply stop taking many ADHD medications, but for some it's better to taper off slowly. You need to tell your doctor that you would like to stop the medication so you can have a conversation. Sometimes your doctor can adjust the medication to reduce the bothersome side effects. After you stop the medication, you must decide whether to try a different one.

The same problems that made you decide to try medication in the first place may still be there—a major reason to try a different medication. However, your experience with the medication may be unpleasant enough that you decide to try a different treatment approach.

Dr. Sarah Says   People are constantly asking me for the best medication with the fewest side effects. If there were just one, my job would be super easy. But there are many medications on the market, because there is no one medication that is best for everyone. People respond to medication very individually. One person can think a particular medication is fantastic, while another person, even if it is his sister, might think it is terrible. But she can let her doctor know what happened and ask to try something else.

Do Supplements Work?

Many vitamins and supplements have been marketed for ADHD. It would be great if they worked well, but for most people, at best they work a little bit. Here is what you need to know:

- Vitamins and supplements generally are not approved or regulated by the Food and Drug Administration (FDA).

- Anybody can manufacture and market a supplement, and what it says on the box or jar is not necessarily exactly what is in the pills inside.

- Supplements can claim some health benefits on the basis of limited or inconclusive evidence, rather than the strict standards the FDA holds for medication approval.

There is a "medical food supplement" called Vayarin, an omega fatty acid product, that must be taken for several months before any effect can be seen. Vayarin is a "medical food" made from ingredients that receive the FDA's Generally Recognized as Safe (GRAS) designation. To earn this, the product's safety and efficacy must be confirmed with scientific evidence. Dr. Sarah is not impressed with Vayarin.

What Kind of Doctors Prescribe ADHD Meds?

This really can be confusing. It depends on who in your community tends to do this kind of prescribing and whether your general practitioner is comfortable with prescribing. Here's a general listing of different doctors and how they can help.

- Pediatricians, family medicine doctors, and internists—the general care doctors that you see for your regular medical care—can prescribe ADHD medications.

- Specialists like pediatric or adult psychiatrists or neurologists can be seen on referral from pediatricians and family medicine doctors for treatment options for ADDYTeens.

- Psychologists and other therapists (LMFTs, LCSWs) offer talk therapy, with weekly sessions in which you explore how to respond to and manage your situations. One major therapy type is cognitive behavioral therapy (CBT). They do not prescribe medication.

- Psychiatrists can both provide therapy and prescribe medication; some focus solely on medication.

Which doctor is right for you? Well, most people start with their regular doctors. You might ask your general care doctor whether they are comfortable diagnosing ADHD. Some of these doctors might not do the diagnosing part, but if you have been diagnosed elsewhere, they may feel comfortable either starting or continuing medications for you.

Whether you see a specialist may depend on what is usual in your community. In some communities and regions, ADHD specialists are hard to find. Specialists generally can take more time per patient than general medical doctors can, which is helpful in getting an accurate diagnosis. They often feel very comfortable in managing ADHD with medication, either just to start you out or on an ongoing basis. Most commonly psychiatrists prescribe and manage these medications, but many neurologists do too. Again, some psychiatrists will also do talk therapy; others just focus on medication management.

Psychologists are PhDs, not MDs. You may or may not see a psychologist as part of your ADHD evaluation and treatment. Psychologists do different types of talk therapy. They may evaluate whether you have ADHD by discussing with you how you think and behave. They may help you manage the ADHD by helping you become aware of when you are focused and when you are not, and what being focused feels like. They also may help you set goals, organize, and work on your self-esteem. Some psychologists also do *neuropsych testing*, or *educational testing*, which can include testing your IQ, academic achievement, and how well you focus. Testing can sometimes be helpful, but it can be expensive and often is not necessary. Other therapists who do talk therapy, like LMFTs and LCSWs, have training in counseling but not as extensively as PhDs.

How to Talk with Your Doctor

Remember, ADDYTeens, you are the star of this particular show. Your voice matters most in this discussion. You are the best person to explain what is going on inside your head. Doctors and parents cannot read your mind. They do not go to school with you or experience your relationships with your friends. Please speak up during the visit! Make your voice heard! If you let your parents do all the talking, the doctor will hear what *they* think is going on, not what *you* think is going on.

Ideally, your doctor can communicate well with you. However, communication is a two-way street. It's more than OK to ask your doctor basic questions. Your doctor would love to answer them, because it's important to them that you understand what is going on.

Sometimes you might feel that a doctor is giving you a hard time because they are asking, "Why didn't you do your homework?" Here is what you need to understand:

- Your doctor would like to hear your honest answers and is (we hope) just trying to better understand you and how you think.

- Your doctor is *not* interested in punishing you for scoring poorly on tests or not doing your work.

- Your doctor *is* interested in getting a vivid picture of how you function in different situations. It's helpful to be honest with both the doctor and yourself.

- Having your parents there can be helpful, because they have a perspective on you that is different from your own. How others view you can be different from how you view yourself.

Doctors are all individuals who communicate in different ways. Most doctors understand how ADHD works and recognize that it is a valid diagnosis. A few (often older) doctors may find the entire concept of ADHD diagnosis hard to accept—some medical prejudice lingers. Try to avoid these doctors. If your family doctor is one of them, enlist your parents to help you find a more receptive one. Some doctors communicate with ADDYTeens at their level; others talk down to them. This is not acceptable; if it happens, find another doctor. Some doctors don't answer questions as well as others do. Be sure you go to someone who can effectively communicate with you.

Consider possible medications by weighing the benefits with any possible side effects. Ask your doctor what you can expect from each suggested medication. Ask if it must be taken every day or if you can skip it on weekends. How long do the effects typically last each day? Many ADHD medications wear off after a certain number of hours during the day. What happens if you don't like the medication? Many doctors try a low dose first, hoping to avoid side effects. However, after taking the medication you may find it doesn't work for you, because for you an effective dose must be higher.

Take Action The most important question that you can ask you doctor is how best to communicate. Some doctors require visits in order to adjust medications. Others do so via email or phone. Don't be afraid to let your doctor know when the medication is not working out. You should not have to wait weeks to make adjustments.

Ask your doctor:

* Is there an office email service that you can use?

* Will this channel be separate and private from your parents' communication with the doctor?

* How soon can you expect to get a reply to your messages?

* If you are on medication, ask about the best way to get it filled at the pharmacy. This is especially important for college students, who may be living far from home.

Private Issues and Your Doctor

There may be times when you are reluctant to tell your doctor certain things. Or you may worry whether the doctor will get you into trouble with your parents. Or your parents may even be in the room. For example, you may be worried to share that:

- You smoke marijuana, drink alcohol, or take other drugs.

- You feel anxious or depressed.

- Getting fantastic grades or going to college is not actually your goal.

Any of these might be embarrassing for you to tell your doctor, because you don't know how your doctor will react. And you may not want your parents to know.

Most doctors will talk to their ADDYTeen patients privately for at least part of the evaluation time. Make sure your doctor knows that you'd like to talk privately. You can call the doctor in advance to make sure you get private time, or during the visit request to speak privately without your parents. What you talk about will be confidential if you tell the doctor you want this protection. Your parents will not find out what you talk about with the doctor unless the doctor feels you are in imminent danger and your parents must be informed for your safety and survival.

Share Your M&M's—Not Your Medication

We're going to keep this simple because it is simple:

- Do *not* take anyone else's ADHD medication. It's stupid, and dangerous.

- Do *not* share your ADHD medication. It's stupid, and dangerous.

Now, read these two points again, and again. OK? Got it?

Some ADDYTeens share or buy medications (or other substances) from friends, but you really should not take *any* medications unless you are thoroughly checked out by a doctor. Some people are not good candidates for medication—and you may not know if you are one of them without a doctor's expertise.

You could have side effects that you and your friends may not know how to handle. Doses may need to be adjusted. The ADHD medication could interact dangerously with other medications someone is taking.

ADHD Medication and Addiction Risks

One big fear of many ADDYTeens, and particularly their parents, is that taking medications will lead to addiction, because the FDA classifies all stimulants as addictive. Parents think their child will be given "speed," because some ADHD medications are amphetamine based.

Here is what you need to know:

- These are not street drugs. They are carefully regulated. They are given under a doctor's care.

- ADHD medications are highly unlikely to be addictive when used at the doses doctors typically prescribe for ADHD. At high doses, however—beyond what doctors prescribe for ADHD—the medications can be addictive.

- Many ADDYTeens take ADHD medications Monday through Friday only, or don't take them while on summer or winter break, without any withdrawal or other problems.

- Many ADDYTeens prefer not to take their medication when they don't need it to study or perform in an exam or competition—which should reassure you that addiction is not a big factor with ADHD medications. For example, I don't take my medication unless I need it for studying, and I don't take it while on vacation.

ADDYTeens also ask Dr. Sarah whether these medications are gateway drugs. No! ADDYTeens using stimulant medications are not more or less likely to abuse illicit drugs. In fact, if you have managed your ADHD well, with or without medications, you are much less likely to do illicit drugs than an ADDYTeen with undertreated or untreated ADHD. The better you are functioning, the less likely you are to abuse any sort of substance.

Sadly, many of us who have not learned how to win with ADHD wind up self-medicating with more addicting drugs in an effort to feel better or escape from the challenges of living with ADHD.

Bottom line: we believe that the ADHD medications, if used properly, *prevent* significantly more addiction problems than they create. They work well for most of us. The side effects are easily managed, and proper diet and exercise reduces their impact.

ADHD and Marijuana

ADDYTeens: We are not judging, just sharing. So read this carefully. Here is what you need to know:

- Don't think of marijuana as harmless. Many ADDYTeens consider marijuana a "natural" substance and without side effects. That is not true for anybody. Marijuana is a substance that goes into your brain, and anybody can experience side effects.

- Marijuana is not an FDA-approved ADHD medication. Marijuana use among ADDYTeens is growing by leaps and bounds, and there are many articles online touting its benefits. However, it has not undergone rigorous scientific study, and for many people it may not work well. Marijuana may provide some benefits for focusing—particularly from its antianxiety effects—but there are also potential side effects. Many are concerned that marijuana can lead to addiction as a "gateway" drug.

- Over time, heavy, intense, and chronic marijuana use, especially in ADDYTeens, can lower your IQ score and possibly reduce motivation and increase depression. Read this twice. The last thing ADDYTeens need less of is motivation.

- Remember, everything in life has consequences, and it's important to try to understand all aspects of a choice before making it. These are your choices. Choose wisely.

chapter 8

Your Choices: Choose Wisely

So you've made it to the last chapter. Woo-hoo! We have covered a lot of concepts, coaching ideas, and Plays that all contribute to how we manage and ultimately win with our ADHD.

There is no doubt that ADHD impacts our lives; what really matters is how we manage it. Do we get upset and anxious over it? Or do we find a way to become our best selves in spite of it?

It is time to move beyond discussing the concepts and the coaching and our Plays. It is time to make some choices.

ADDYTeens: without effort, there is no success. We must push ourselves to win and become the best we can be. This is our job and no one else's.

Here is what you need to know:

- Winning with ADHD is not a one-step process; it is a lifelong process.

- ADHD doesn't go away; winning is a matter of how you manage and deal with it to the best of your ability over time.

- Managing your ADHD takes time and effort—period. Winning in life takes time and effort—period.

This chapter is about the choices that lie ahead as you grow up, get smarter, and become more and more capable of taking charge of your life. The goal of this book is to equip you to become independent, responsible, and goal oriented, and to help you get started taking action toward your goals.

Real talk:

- We must take it upon ourselves to take ownership of our life.

- We must go above and beyond to better ourselves; just meeting the minimum is not enough.

- We must strive to reach our personal best.

- It is up to you to decide how you want to distinguish yourself.

It took me years and so many tears to finally feel comfortable with my own ADHD—my mind, the way I acted, the way I spoke, and how I dealt with external factors around me like school, friends, and family. Over many years, I have given much thought to what success and winning with ADHD is for me— what it looks like and how break it down so I could take action. I had to look at the big picture and ask myself: *What do I want out of my life?*

My answer: *I want to win.* I just needed to do it.

With any kind of ADHD, there is a formula to success. My formula has four factors:

Grit + Medication + Guidance + Support

All four factors are in play. All must be addressed in some way for you to achieve success and win with your ADHD. You must choose how you want to make use of these four domains and decide how you want to take action. Here is the percentage of each factor we think applies for ADDYTeens.

Grit—35 Percent

"Grit" means courage and resolve; strength of character. Grit is the measure of a person's ability to accept difficulty, deal with challenging circumstances, and persevere through obstacles when faced with fear or lack of confidence. Those of us with ADHD can think of grit as a combination of acceptance (that our ADHD is very real, and very unfair in some situations) and resilience in overcoming the challenges involved in managing our ADHD.

Grit is required to win with your ADHD, but grit may not come naturally to some. Rather, it is something you develop over time by controlling the controllables, practicing the Plays, and learning to let go of disappointment when things don't go the way you planned or hoped. The concepts and coaching sections in this book—You and Your ADHD, Managing Your ADHD, Managing Your Time, Speaking Up for Yourself—all require you to decide how you want to deal with ADHD's complications and demands.

At some point you have to ask yourself: *Should I see my ADHD as an obstacle too difficult to overcome, or as a challenge that makes me stronger?*

Each concept explored in this book can guide you through specific life situations and provide you steps to overcome and conquer whatever comes your way. It's up to you how you want to apply these ideas and take action.

- Will you choose to take the extra steps to limit distractions—going to your teacher's office hours to ask questions, talking it out with that friend who pushes your buttons, and correcting your own behavior?

- Will you suit up—even when you are afraid or unsure—to reach your goals?

- Are you willing to work hard—very hard, harder than your friends—to overcome obstacles, no matter how big or small?

- Are you willing to run with a backpack heavy with rocks to make your personal best time even though your friends without ADHD often run faster and win more often?

Now, how will you choose to develop and practice grit? Take action!

- Do you want opportunities to pass you by because you fear rejection, failure, or challenges?

- Do you want to get an A in the class by advocating for yourself, or slide by because you don't want to seem annoying and uncool for asking questions?

- Are you willing to have to spend another hour on your homework because your family is being loud in the living room, or will you decide to speak up to better your concentration?

I have asked myself these questions over the years. It wasn't easy always having to push myself when faced with an obstacle. Sure, at first sometimes I gave up, but mostly I suited up. Over time all of this became ingrained habits. Speaking up for what I needed in times of doubt, triple-checking my work with my teachers, and making friends with new people become easier over time. Now I'm ready to try, to stretch to new heights, to win.

ADHD can definitely make life a bit challenging, but with grit comes determination, effort, and progress.

Medication—20 Percent

Medication helps those with learning and attention issues gain traction and feel more confident starting and finishing tasks. Medication does not make you smart, or good at school, or more persuasive, friendly, or charming. Medication is like cleats for a soccer player—it gives you traction. It does not make you a better player. Think about it: you can play soccer without cleats, but it's just harder than it should be, and you probably won't play your best.

We've discussed how medication is only a partial solution to the challenge of ADHD. Choose to take medication or not; either way, you still need to focus and attend to important tasks, regardless of distractions. I've mentioned that I don't take my medication every day, only when I need it the most. I decide when and what dose of medication to take. These are my choices. But making these choices wasn't always easy.

Figuring out whether medication is right for you is a matter of caring for your body and openly communicating with your doctor and your family. There are many different paths to improving your concentration and limiting impulsiveness. Whatever choices you make, it is wise to have an honest conversation with your family and doctor. Your body and mind work hard every day—if you feel like something is off, it's time for an honest and open dialogue.

Remember that you are in control of what you put in your body. Not your parents or your friends. *You.* No one else is a better judge of what your body needs or doesn't need. Speaking up for what you need and taking action about these issues can be daunting and scary at times. You must decide how you want to tackle self-care and advocacy.

Medication is not the golden ticket to winning with ADHD. But if you needed glasses to read and study, would you choose not to use them? What steps are you willing to take?

Guidance—25 Percent

At the beginning of this book, I shared a story about jumping into the hole to teach my friend how to get out. Well, friend, here we are. I have shared how I got out of the hole. Will you choose to take my guidance? Will you listen to Dr. Sarah?

The Plays offered in this book were a big part of what has made me a success. But you too have coaches, teachers, directors, therapists, and parents to help guide you through tough situations and provide you with the skills to make progress on your own time. Will you choose to listen?

Accepting guidance is a very important skill for you to master. Finding someone from whom you can learn ideas, tricks, and skills can improve your ability to tackle challenges or fears, learn more about yourself, and gain the confidence to be independent.

When you take guidance—like this book, a podcast, a lecture, or a face-to-face conversation—and apply what you've learned to your own life, real magic happens. Dr. Sarah, my professors, colleagues, and my family help me become a better person every day. Who guides you?

Guidance works in two directions.

- Guidance is offered—you choose whether to listen or ignore it.

- Guidance is sought—when you ask for help and advice.

I have learned to ask for help and advice. When I was fourteen, thinking about my ADHD, I decided to learn more. I chose to ask for advice. I needed guidance. Let's face it: we don't know everything. Sometimes we can get stubborn, assume we *do* know everything, and feel frustrated when we lose traction or get stuck.

Part of winning with ADHD is knowing when to ask for help, when to listen to your friends and family, and when to advocate for more resources when you need them. We've discussed and practiced these concepts throughout the book, and I have coached you with Plays. Now you need to choose whom to ask for help.

What does reaching out look like in real life?

If you wanted to perfect a soccer move, of course you would ask your soccer coach for help. Asking an expert to share their knowledge will expand your personal growth.

If you forget the steps to a math formula, you can choose to ask your teacher for help. There is no shame in getting extra help to improve your game (and your grades), so why not ask a math expert?

When I wanted to learn more about my ADHD so I could write my first book—*Embracing Your ADHD*—I took action. I was just fourteen. I went to a lecture conducted by Dr. Stephen Hinshaw, a world-famous scientist and expert on ADHD. I listened, I took notes, and though the lecture was complex, I learned a great deal. After the lecture, I asked him for help in how to approach writing a book on ADHD. His guidance was so helpful to me, and he still gives me guidance today; in fact, he wrote the foreword to this book. But I had to ask in the first place.

Think about it. Will you choose to ask for guidance?

Asking for help doesn't mean you're dumb or weak. It means that you are willing to try something new and willing to think and learn before taking action. Earlier in the book we discussed what being impulsive means. Asking for guidance is the opposite of being impulsive.

What steps are you willing to take to make proactive change in your life? You choose.

Support—20 Percent

Family support plays a major part in developing our ability to accept, thrive, and win with our ADHD. But family may not be the only support system you need or want. Some of us have no family. Some of us may not have family we can rely on. So let's call it your *team*. It may include friends; teachers; your rabbi, priest, imam, or pastor; and a coach or counselor. As with most sports, you need a team whose members work together and support each other no matter how hard times get.

We've discussed ADHD at home, managing responsibilities, speaking up to your parents for what you need, and practicing open communication with your team members. In some teams these skills come easily; in other families, we must work harder.

ADHD can often put a strain on us and other family and team members. However, we must remember that we are not our ADHD. We have the power to choose how to act, how to communicate, how to take needed space when we're getting emotional, and how to reach out for help. These are skills required in life, whether you have ADHD or not.

Having team support means knowing that others understand your backpack is full of rocks, that you are not perfect, and that it's your effort and your grit that matter most. It is having people believe in you when you might not believe in yourself. It is knowing that if things don't go well this time, you will get encouragement about the next time. It is all those around you who lift you up when times are hard, and celebrate with you when things go well.

And you need to return the favor: we ADDYTeens play an important role in our own family and on our team. On your soccer or basketball team, can you expect to start in the game after not putting that much effort into practice? *Hmm.* That wouldn't seem fair or realistic. Same thing goes for our family and our team. If we want our team's support, trust, and effort, we must give the same to them.

How Will You Win with Your ADHD?

That is the question we hope you are asking yourself now. Will you start to take action? How are you going to do it?

These questions imply hope. Yes, *you* can do it. Yes, *you* can be a winner.

However, answering those questions also relies on *you* suiting up. How are you going to win? We have demonstrated through the Plays how you can approach studying for an exam or talking to your teachers, parents, and friends, step by step. These step-by-step Plays function to show you that breaking down a big task into small chunks is the easiest and simplest way to tackle any situation you run into. We hope that our playbook will help you, but in the end, you know yourself. Understand who you are. Accept yourself as yourself. Don't try for perfection. Try for improvement—every day.

How will you win with your ADHD? The great part is, you define your own success. You define winning as making the improvements you want to make. You define winning as doing your personal best and making progress in managing your ADHD.

Winning is no fun without celebration. So when you win, celebrate. Winning is wonderful. Go do it!